MANAGING YOUR COMMITMENT

BRING LASTING PASSION, PURPOSE, AND SUCCESS BY DOING WHAT YOU SAID YOU WOULD DO LONG AFTER YOU SAID YOU WOULD DO IT!

MIKE DRIGGERS

Mike Driggers / IME Publishing Group
362 willowcreek ln
Martinez, Ca. 94553
www.ManagingYourCommitmentToSuccess.com
www.IMEPublishingGroup.com

Warning—Disclaimer
*The purpose of this book is to educate and inspire. This book is not
intended to give advice or make promises or guarantees that anyone following the ideas, tips, suggestions, techniques or strategies
will have the same results as the people listed throughout the stories
contained herein. The author, publisher and distributor(s) shall have
neither liability nor responsibility to anyone with respect to any loss
or damage caused, or alleged to be caused, directly or indirectly by
the information contained in this book.*

Ordering Information:
Quantity sales. Special discounts are available on quantity purchases
by corporations, associations, and others. For details, contact the
"Special Sales Department" at the ad-dress above.

Managing Your Commitment/ Mike Driggers. —2nd ed.
ISBN 978-0-692-25930-6

WHAT OTHERS ARE SAYING ABOUT MIKE DRIGGERS AND HIS STRATEGIES

If you're ready to positively transform your life, Then read and absorb the strategies in this brilliant book by my friend Mike Driggers! Mike Truly cares about helping others and his ideas will make a positive difference in your life!" — **James Malinchak**, Featured on ABCs Hit TV Show, "Secret Millionaire" The Author of the Top-Selling Book, Millionaire Success Secrets Founder, www.BigMoneySpeaker.com

Recommend To All Leaders – Great Insights!
— **Daniel Eugene** "Rudy" Ruettiger, Played football for University of Notre Dame and In 1993, TRISTAR Productions immortalized his life story with the blockbuster film, "RUDY"

Mike Driggers principles offer a fresh and timely perspective that will ignite your soul and put fuel on your internal fire to go out and be the best you can be in your personal and professional life. — **Jill Lublin**, CEO, PublicityCrashCourse.com, International Speaker & 4x Best selling Author

Whether you're a seasoned business leader, a recent graduate just starting your career or an entrepreneur, Mike Driggers principles and approach apply across all Industries and disciplines. Mike's attitude is inspiring and he is an outstanding mentor. — **Jonathan Atkinson**, Criminal Investigator Santa Clara County District Attorney's Office

Mike's ideologies to achieving everything you ever wanted in business and in Life gives you a step-by-step blueprint that will make you strive harder and push further than you ever have.— **Sonia Hinojo**, Air Liquide Sales and Marketing Manager

GREAT meeting today--as usual, terrific atmosphere for connecting, and a great tactics and strategy exercise led by Mike. — **David Hirata**, Theatrical Modern Magician

I really appreciate the high quality of biz coaching my group has from Mike Driggers! — **Ellen Vaughn Simonin**, Physical Therapist and Acupuncturist

Mike's practical ways to becoming a high achiever in business and in your personal life through his simple to use principles are a must-have and I highly recommend you learn them now. — **Greg Kite,Former** NBA Player for the Boston Celtics & Executive Field Chairman for Hegemon Group International

The ideas presented by Mike Driggers offer an inspiration and exciting perspective that will change the course of how you succeed in business or life. — **Steve Jones**, 10 years Law Enforcement

Whether you're an executive at a fortune 500 company or an entrepreneur Mike Driggers solutions go far beyond traditional business practices. Any organization can put this to immediate use and achieve amazing results. — **Steve Aust**, Former NBA Player for the Los Angeles Lakers, Chairman Co-Founder of Agora Advantage

Mike Driggers strategies are remarkable and insightful. He provides an easy-to-understand blueprint that makes you want to jump ahead and implement his process immediately. — **Belza López**, Housing Specialist for the City of Napa

Mike Driggers Concepts will become an invaluable tool in business and life for those who are on a pursuit of Excellence and Success. — **Gabriela Aguilera**, Orthodontic Treatment Coordinator

PROCRASTINATION KILLER
Special **FREE** Bonus Gift For **YOU!**

To help you stand out from the crowd
FREE BONUS RESOURCE for you at;
www.theprocrastinationkiller.com/procrastinationgift

Get your FREE Report And You'll Discover...

1. The Top 5 most common signs of chronic procrastinators (It could be YOU!)

2. The reasons why you're terribly UNPRODUCTIVE!

3. Your inner power to push through any procrastination pitfall

**www.theprocrastinationkiller.com/
procrastinationgift**

Managing Your Commitment

"Share This Book"

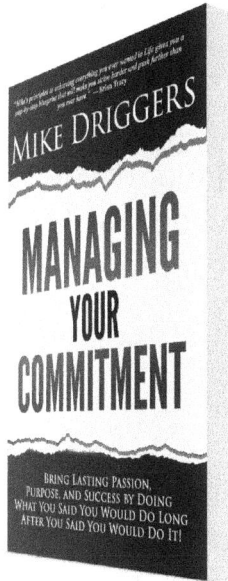

Retail 17.95

Special Quantity Discounts

5-20 Books	15.95
21-99 books	13.95
100-499 books	11.95
500-999 books	9.95
1,000 + books	8.95

To Order Go To www.BookMikeToday.com

THE IDEAL PROFESSIONAL SPEAKER FOR Your NEXT EVENT!

Any organization that wants to develop and grow their business to become "extraordinary" needs to hire Mike for a keynote and /or workshop training!

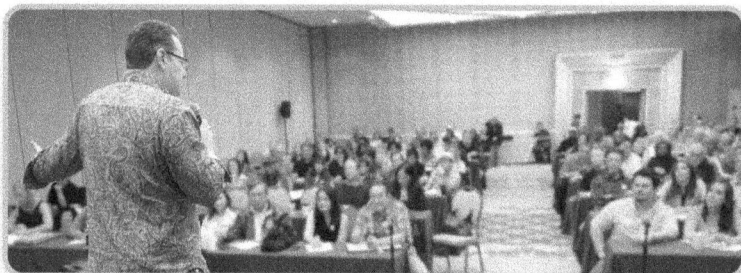

TO CONTACT OR BOOK MIKE TO SPEAK:
IME Publishing Group

(866) 7BOOKME

(866) 726-6563

www.BookMikeToday.com

Info@BookMikeToday.com

DEDICATION

This book is dedicated to everyone who wants to make a drastic and positive change in their lives. We've all had goals that we failed to reach and most of us have struggled to make ends meet at one time or another. But, as we all know, it's not how many times you're knocked down that counts; it's how many times you get back up. Hopefully, this book will get you off the canvas and back into the fight.

I would like to thank my Mom and Dad for their continued support, as well as my fiancé Gaby Aguilera for being part of the publishing process. Special thanks go out to my kids Alex, Daniel and Arianna. All of you are a blessing in my life and definitely keep me motivated to be the best father I can be.

After you've read this book, please let me know how your journey goes. I look forward to hearing your success story and sharing it with those who read my succeeding books.

"You don't get paid for the hour. You get paid for the value that you bring to that hour."

— Jim Rohn

CONTENTS

INTRODUCTION

How would you measure your success in life? Are you living the lifestyle you always dreamed about or are you struggling to make the rent payment? Are you driving a clunker that you pray won't break down on the way to your next job interview? When you look into your refrigerator, do you see only expired yogurts and packets of ketchup and hot sauce? Do you open your bank statement and read nothing but zeroes in front of the decimal? Or is it just simply feeling as if your life has come to a stalemate?

Face it, you've made some very poor decisions during your life and the result is a messy and uncertain existence.

To make things worse, the world is changing at lightning speed and the further behind you get the harder it is to catch up. Not since the Great Depression have people had to fend for themselves in such a thin job market. More folks are starting their own businesses and crossing their fingers, hoping they have what it takes to survive the economic downturn.

For many of us, the time is now to hit the Delete button on old habits that fail to produce positive results. You may find yourself at a plateau in life or you may have actually hit rock bottom as you read this but the good news is you've taken the first step to the top.

Believe me, I know what it feels like to be in the rock bottom position. I have been through some tough times myself; everything from divorce to almost bankruptcy to lossing a company. Struggle was my middle name so I am serious when I say that I am on your side.

It's possible for you to overcome your self-doubt by mastering the techniques in this book. Along the journey you'll find better ways to manage your time, resources and relationships to build a solid foundation for the future. It's not rocket science but it will take commitment on your part and a determination that you may not be accustomed to.

Have you ever considered how much more successful you could be in life if you were able to put absolutely everything you have into your efforts? Not 25% or 50%, but 100% of you into achieving your goals!

What would you Accomplish?

While you consider this important question, think about this. Not many overachievers point to their exceptional abilities as the main reason for their success; instead they credit their ability to master self-discipline!

They consider this mastery of self-discipline the "missing ingredient" that broke them free from the pack and created the edge that helped them turn their dreams into reality.

This is a secret you won't read about very often because it takes real hard work to take advantage of. On the other hand, the rewards can be enormous.

If you do the work that I encourage you to do, you will see the same results, or better, compared to people with "exceptional" talent. It's how the rules of the world operate. Once you employ these rules, you can:

- Stop eating mindlessly and packing on fat.

- Free up the time to exercise and build a body you're proud of.

- Make more money in ways you find rewarding, not degrading.

- Break down barriers that keep you from communicating with interesting people.

- Develop the confidence that comes with keeping promises to yourself.

That's just the tip of the iceberg. As you build self-discipline, every single area of your life—mental, physical, spiritual and financial—will benefit. All of it.

By the time you're through with this book, you'll have all the tools you need to grow from being a "wanter" and "wisher" to being a "an achiever", or a high performer.

I couldn't be happier to take this journey with you. There's no better feeling than knowing that you've helped someone turn bad habits that hold them back into good habits that breed success.

Some of my suggestions and observations may seem harsh. Just know I have your best interests at heart. Chances are you've been stuck in neutral for far too long. A little shock may be what's needed to get you moving forward quickly.

Let's team up so you can learn how to Manage your Commitment and build your future success.

Mike

1

THE FIVE D'S

"One setback is one setback—not the end of the world,
nor is it the end of your journey toward a better you."
— Jillian Michaels

When you look at your current level of success, does it feel like you're falling further behind as each day goes by? If you pay any attention to your bank statements and investment portfolio, you may conclude that your career has been a complete failure and you're going nowhere fast.

The new world is changing quickly so now is the best time to regroup and make a positive move forward. But, as the title of the book says, you need to manage your commitment. This is not an easy fix, especially if you continue to place roadblocks in your own path.

You need a new approach to how you view your work and personal life. This new approach takes into account five critical "D" factors:

1. **Definition**—What improvements are you looking to commit to? Are they for your career or your personal life? You need to outline the goals you plan to reach through your new commitment.

2. **Dedication**—Learning new things is not always easy but you have to stay current if you're going to compete in the modern world. Dedicate yourself to a new training regimen or establish a meaningful mentor relationship.

3. **Desire**—Even people who hate their jobs can work hard. So, that's not always the answer. The key is, do you wake up every morning with the fire in your belly to take on the next challenge?

4. **Drive**—In order to succeed, you'll need to push yourself through some serious hurdles. Ordinary people find excuses to quit when they encounter these obstacles. Do you have the strength to push through?

5. **Do**—The people who win are the ones who do. The people who lose are those who continue with their old way of thinking, make excuses or find others to blame. These are the folks who give up at the slightest hint of a challenge.

Although no one ever figures it out completely, I have discovered enough of the winning formula to pass it on to you. Managing Your Commitment is a lifestyle, not an overnight occurrence. But, if you follow my guidelines, I guarantee that you'll advance from the depths of an unproductive and unrewarding life to the limitless heights of success.

MIKE DRIGGERS

2

DOWN ON YOUR LUCK?

"People will choose unhappiness over uncertainty."
— Timothy Ferriss

The last thing I want to see is you being discouraged about where you currently find yourself. Many others have found themselves in much more dire straits and bounced back to taste unbounded success. I want you to be the next success story.

In fact, you may be surprised when you read about these extremely successful individuals who were once down on their luck. Like you, they had to overcome failure and physical setbacks that could've stopped them in their tracks.

Instead, they all got back up.

Bill Gates was a business failure

That's right, the richest person in the world saw his first company, Traf-O-Data, fail miserably. When Gates and his partner, Paul Allen, tried to sell it, the product wouldn't even work. Gates and Allen didn't let that stop them from trying again, though. I believe you've heard of Microsoft?

Jim Carrey was on the streets

When he was 15, Carrey was forced to drop out of school to support his family. His father was an unemployed musician and the family eventually had to live in a van. Carrey didn't let this stop him from achieving his dream. He went from having his dad drive him to comedy clubs to becoming one of the highest paid actors in Hollywood.

Stephen King faced rejection

If it weren't for his wife, "Carrie" may not have ever been filmed. After being consistently rejected by publishers, King gave up and threw his first book in the trash. His wife retrieved the manuscript and urged King to finish it. Now his books have sold 350 million copies and have been made into countless major motion pictures.

Kris Carr beats cancer

In 2003, Karr was diagnosed with Stage IV cancer. Instead of succumbing to the disease, Carr attacked her cancer with a brand new nutritional lifestyle and turned her experience into a series of successful self-help books and documentaries. Eventually, she launched her own wellness website and is now revered as one of the most prominent experts on healthy living.

MIKE DRIGGERS

3

SET YOUR COMMITMENTS

"Life is like a game of chess. To win you have to make a move." — Alan Rufus

There are many different types of commitments and degrees of intention. The depth of the commitment and the meaning behind it aren't as important initially as just creating a habit and a means of following through on what you said you would accomplish.

If you decide that you want to sail around the world and you want to accomplish that by the time you're 50 years old, get started on the path toward that commitment. Enjoy the process to get there and enjoy the reward of your trip around the world.

If you decide that you want to renovate your kitchen or clean out your garage, that can be just as important. It's a simpler commitment to achieve and it may not have the lasting joy and rewards that sailing around the world may have. But when all is said and done, honoring your commitments leads to the same results:

- You create a habit of success

- You develop personal pride

- You become a person whom people trust and look up to

- You attract success and opportunities

- You attract supportive people and you become the type of person who is engaged and supportive of others

- Your relationships are stronger and the world around you has more meaning and purpose

- Life is more fulfilling

Honoring your commitments can be simple and doing so has huge and lasting implications. Learn to set the right commitments that honor who you are and what you want to accomplish in your life.

4

YOU HAVE TO GET IT YOURSELF!

"It was character that got us out of bed,
commitment that moved us into action, and
discipline that enabled us to follow through."
— Zig Ziglar

LIFE IS LIKE A CAFETERIA

Long ago a man came to America from Eastern Europe. After being processed at Ellis Island, he went into a cafeteria to get something to eat. He sat down at an empty table and waited for someone to take his order. Of course, nobody did. Finally, a woman with a tray of food sat down opposite him and informed him how a cafeteria worked.

"Start out at that end," she said. "Just go along the line and pick out what you want. At the other end they'll tell you how much you have to pay."

"I soon learned that's how everything works in America," the man later told a friend. "You can get anything you want as long as you are willing to pay the price to get it."

"You can even get success," he continued. "But you'll never get it if you wait for someone to bring it to you. You have to get up and get it yourself."

The word commitment is often thrown around carelessly. For example, a new hire may say, "I'm committed to making ABC company the best widget company on the market." Someone striving to lose weight might say, "I'm committed to getting healthy and working out."

Of course we're all familiar with the relationship version of commitment. "I'll always be there for you, baby."

These statements all have something in common. No, it's not that they're false promises. Their commonality has more to do with the nature of the statements.

When you look at each statement you can see that they are all merely *intentions*.

- The employee *intends* to work hard to make ABC company the best widget company on the market.

- The overweight person *intends* to get healthy and lose weight.

- The boyfriend or girlfriend *intends* to stay with their partner and be faithful.

But as you should know, there's a huge difference between an **_intention_** and an **_outcome_**.

An intention is similar to a dream. It's what you want to be true, what you wish were true, and what you hope will happen. It's the truth in the moment. People often have good intentions and they make commitments based on them. However, it's the depth of their commitment that determines the outcome and when it comes to that there are many depths.

On the other hand, the outcome is the reality. It's what happens when action is taken, promises are kept, and the intention is set in motion through goals, steps and activity.

Intentions are great. They're the spark of what can be. If you have a strong commitment to something—if it is part of who you are and is ingrained into every cell of your body, every breath you take, and every action you make the outcome will reflect the commitment. Your intention will become your reality.

The question is, how do you ensure you're making the right intentions? How do you persevere? How do you honor what you said you'd honor and follow through?

The secret isn't really a secret at all. Following through on your intention is all about desire, integrity, hard work, fortitude and perseverance.

A TALE OF TWO COMMITMENTS

Al and Theresa each want to start a business. Al spends time assessing his strengths and weaknesses. He realizes that, because he's working a traditional 9-to-5 job, it's going to take him some time to launch his business properly.

He creates a business plan and action steps that can be built upon gradually. He's given himself one full year from commitment day to the launch of his business.

He even builds a few months of part-time work into the plan so that he can still earn an income while growing his business to where it can financially sustain him.

Theresa has a completely different approach to the concept of starting a business. She signs up for the occasional business class and attends online seminars. She reads books about starting a business and talks about it incessantly. Unfortunately, Theresa doesn't follow through and never really takes decisive action to turn her "commitment" into a reality.

Al follows through, taking consistently planned and decisive actions to turn his commitment into his reality.

Not surprisingly, their outcomes are quite different. Al now has a thriving business. He has plenty of customers, which allowed him to quit his 9-to-5 job and live his ideal lifestyle. It was a difficult year filled with many sacrifices but, because Al created a commitment that was true to him, his values, and his purpose, he was able to persevere.

Theresa is left with a huge collection of books and not much more. She actually wound up spending more on learning to start a business than Al spent actually starting one. She still works at her day job and has not taken any tangible steps towards her intention to start a business.

As is usually the case, you get out of life what you put into it. However, in order to be able to give your full attention and focus to any commitment, it has to be the right intention for you. It's important to be aware of who you are and what is best suited for you. This first exercise reveals your self-awareness.

STOP!

Action Step #1

Write down intentions that you've made where you haven't experienced the desired outcome. These may be promises that you've made to yourself or others or they may be goals that you didn't achieve.

For example, "I'm going to pay off my debt" is an intention that many people set but never achieve. It's a broken promise to themselves.

Action Step #2

Determine why you didn't achieve your desired outcome. What went wrong? Why didn't it work out?

You might realize that, "I didn't pay off my debt because I didn't create a realistic plan."

Or you might look a little deeper into your emotions, fears and doubts. Be honest with yourself.

You may say to yourself, "I didn't create a realistic debt repayment plan because I was afraid to fail and I didn't want to make the sacrifices required to pay off my debt."

When it comes to identifying commitments—past, present and future—it's essential to understand your potential weaknesses because weaknesses cannot be overcome until they are recognized. Challenges cannot be removed until they are acknowledged.

Once you have a strong grasp of what it means to make a true commitment, you'll be ready to move forward and explore the types of intentions that are right for you at this stage of your life. You'll be poised to make a significant change.

That's what I will focus on in the next chapter. In order to follow through on your promises and commitments, you need to prepare yourself for some drastic changes.

MIKE DRIGGERS

5

JUMPING OUT OF THE JAR

*"The quality of a person's life is in direct propor-
tion to their commitment to excellence, regardless of their chosen field of endeavor."*
— *Vince Lombardi*

RAISE THE ROOF

You train circus fleas by putting them in a jar with a lid on it. When the fleas jump, they will hit the lid again and again as they try to escape. Soon, though, you'll begin to notice something interesting. The fleas continue to jump, but they are no longer jumping high enough to hit the lid.

You can even take the lid off and watch the fleas continue to jump, but they won't jump out of the jar. They have conditioned themselves to jump just so high. Once they've conditioned themselves to jump to that level, that's all they'll ever be able to do.

Many people do the same thing. They create artificial ways to restrict themselves and never even come close to reaching their potential. Just like the fleas, they hit that ceiling and fail to jump higher, thinking they're doing all they can do.

In Chapter 4 I talked about what it means to make a commitment and how so many well-intentioned commitments are eventually abandoned.

I discussed how intention relates to commitment and how the depth of your intention ultimately affects the outcome. If you're deeply committed to something or someone, you'll follow through on the promise you made.

I talked about honesty and why it's important when you're making a commitment. If you're not honest about the reasons for your commitment and the fears you're dealing with, it becomes easier to fail and not follow through on your promise.

On the other hand, facing your doubts and fears will help you establish the right commitments for your hopes and dreams, commitments you can and will follow through on. Commitments you'll feel inspired by, dedicated to and excited about.

Quite often we go through life with ambivalence about the world we live in. We typically fail to look deeply enough at ourselves to recognize the reasons and emotions behind our actions. The only way to truly engage and live in a way that is both rewarding and fulfilling is to take a look deep inside.

I am not saying this will be easy. This may be a drastic step for you but it's time to prepare yourself for change.

HOW ARE FEAR AND DOUBT RELATED?

Fear is like a chain reaction that begins in your brain. A stressful situation presents itself, your brain is stimulated, and it releases chemicals that cause your heart to beat faster. Your mind begins racing and your heart feels as though it's going to pop right out of your chest! Your breathing quickens and your muscles start to react. Your body wants to flee from the situation, a response termed Fight or Flight.

Often, people struggle with self-doubt that's disguised as fear. Can I really do this? Am I good enough? Will the others in the group think I am weak?

STAGE FRIGHT

There's the story about the guitar player who was such a perfectionist that he dreaded taking the stage in front of an audience for fear that he would miss a note and ruin the whole show. During practice sessions, he could be mistaken for Eric Clapton or Carlos Santana, with magic coming out of his fingertips. But put him in a live concert situation and he would go into a severe panic.

He suffered through this for quite a while, long enough that it threatened the future of the band. It took every word of encouragement to finally convince him that no one in the audience could play guitar like he could and they were all there to appreciate his talent, not listen for mistakes.

When he was finally convinced that no one would notice his mistakes, he settled down and turned into the polished guitar player everyone knew he could become and the band still thrives today.

Everything you want is on the other side of fear.
– Jack Canfield

NO STUMBLE BUM

Early in my years I personally experienced this principle. It is a story about a guitar player. At that time I was managing a band that won Star Search back in 80's called the Kingpins. When we were touring I learn this same valuable lesson. When the lead singer was on stage he sometimes forgot the words to the song or played the wrong note. What was interesting is that the only people that realized what had happened was the band and myself. Everyone else had did not even notice. When the lead singer pressed on he acted like there was no mistake and no one noticed. Had he stopped he would have called attention to the mistake and everyone would have realize there what had just happened.

TWO TYPES OF FEAR

Fear of Failure – Unless you learn to overcome the fear of failure, it will take away the ambition and determination that could help you succeed in business and personal endeavors. Instead of living with this fear, ask yourself, "What would I do with my life if I knew I could not fail?"

Fear of the Future – If you have an overwhelming fear of what the future holds, you won't be able to enjoy the present moment. That fear could block you from many successes that you would otherwise realize by living in the moment.

IDENTIFYING YOUR FEARS

Fear is often described as "False Evidence Appearing Real". Fears can become overwhelming if you don't understand why they appear to be so real to you. You can become frustrated with your lack of understanding and keep repeating the fear cycle. If you fail to identify your fears, they may become self-sabotaging. Don't think that unfounded fears can't turn into long-term problems.

Dealing with fear on a constant basis is grueling and tiring. It rules your daily life and your every thought. When you worry unnecessarily or obsess about your fears, it's time to identify them for what they really are. There are common threads that link fears. For example, fear of making a public speech may stem from your fear of rejection.

Extreme fears can cause insecurities that will haunt you day and night until you learn to cope with them. Fear can cause loss of self-esteem which can lead to depression or isolation and other problems that can sabotage your life.

When you face your worst fears, you realize how much they're holding you back. Opportunities simply pass you by when you're so afraid of doing something that you do nothing.

Intellectual, emotional and decision-making abilities are sometimes impaired by fear because it won't let you move outside of your comfort zone and experience new ways of doing and thinking. You'll never live life fully if you can't open yourself up to challenges that can help you grow.

Since fear is usually irrational, you won't make good decisions if you let the fear tie you down and narrow your perspective. It's like trying to remain on the road in the middle of a blinding snowstorm.

Destructive behaviors are also a result of your fears. If you've experienced procrastination, if you neglect even the most basic of responsibilities, and if you doubt yourself at every turn, you probably have a fear linked to success.

After you identify and isolate your fears, study them carefully to determine if they're unfounded or not. Defeating your fears can help rebuild your self-esteem and set you on a much more productive life path.

Opportunities to meet new people, to put yourself in better work situations, or to enhance personal growth can be yours when you learn to work through the resistance.

Joe's Story

Joe started a business as a marketing consultant. He had 20 years of experience in the corporate world and when he was laid off he planned to rally that experience into a business. He assumed he could work for himself and glide into retirement.

However, Joe carried with him a briefcase full of fears and doubts related to a failed business he'd launched shortly after college. He also carried the fears and doubts of his wife, who wanted Joe to look for a "real job."

Needless to say, Joe's second foray into entrepreneurship was also a failure. He caved in to his fears and doubts. His business never got off the ground and he ended up taking another "real job" at a much lower pay rate.

Joe carried the past with him and allowed it to affect his future. Rather than being grateful for the mistakes of the past and learning from them, Joe allowed the errors to cloud his future. They overshadowed every decision he made and every action he took.

If Joe had taken the time to assess where he was right now and to appreciate his strengths and the favorable opportunities presented to him, he would've headed into his new endeavor with more enthusiasm, higher confidence and a total commitment.

Joe would have recognized that his past failure had actually taught him many critical lessons about owning a business. A simple, honest assessment of his strengths, weaknesses, opportunities and threats would've given him all the tools he needed to succeed in his new venture.

He would've had the commitment required to not only succeed but also to demonstrate his untapped potential to his wife. Many failures are just stepping stones to future success.

No doubt, fear of success is real and it can be an obstacle to reaching the top. The good news is that fear can also be re-channeled for great benefit.

DON'T LOOK BACK!

Pastor Joel Osteen of Lakewood Church in Houston once said that your past and future are like the rearview mirror and windshield of your car. When you peer into the tiny rearview mirror, you're looking at where you've been (the past).

However, when you gaze through the much bigger windshield, you're looking at where you're headed (the future).

WRITE THAT BOOK!

How deep do our fears run? For the longest time, the biggest reason I hadn't written the book that was stuck in my brain was that deep down I still actually believed something that was completely impossible: that hidden between my cranium and my keyboard were the magical, perfectly blended words that would wow and fascinate everyone on the planet. Phrases that were so beautifully written that neither friend nor foe would have anything to argue about. A book that would bring everyone together, and that, most importantly, would not cause anyone to write me nastygrams, claim I was crazy, or call me a fool.

You probably know that my goal was unattainable. As the saying goes, if you want everyone to like you, nobody will.

Fear may have been keeping you from taking responsibility for yourself and your actions (or lack of action). Defeating the fears that are causing you to miss life's opportunities will make you even more secure.

When you feel more secure about your emotional well-being, you feel better about facing life's challenges and are open to experiencing personal growth. You'll open your own doors to meet people and socialize, which can lead to many new and exciting opportunities.

This kind of motivation keeps us searching, learning and taking chances. When you identify and face the fears that destroy your motivation, you'll remove the obstacles that keep you from the full enjoyment of life.

DEFEATING YOUR WORST FEARS

It's important to identify our fears, analyze them, and then decide whether they're real or not. Most fears that keep us from realizing success are unfounded. Eliminating your fears involves gradually going into those situations which make you fearful. This is a slow process but, with practice, you will eventually begin to feel less anxious about facing this type of situation and see your fears diminished.

Many heroes from humble or dire beginnings have overcome tremendous fears to accomplish great and important things. Franklin Roosevelt, who overcame many physical obstacles to become the 32nd President of the United States and led us through the darkest days of World War II, inspired a nation in his first inaugural address by saying, "The only thing we have to fear is fear itself."

7 STEPS TO CONQUERING FEAR

Understanding fear and how it works is the first step to overcoming it. The correct path of action is to embrace your decision and create a goal. Take a leap of faith. Trust that you are good enough to see this through.

Build your self-esteem. When you think highly enough of yourself, there's hardly anything that will get you down permanently. Whatever fear you're harboring will fade when you know you have the ability to cope with any problem.

Interrogate yourself. After you've identified and isolated your worst fears, ask yourself a series of questions such as, "What's the worst that can happen?" and, "What can I do to minimize the fear?" These are good ways to pare down the fear to a manageable size.

Do what you're afraid of. A lot has been written about overcoming fear by attacking it head-on. If you're afraid of heights, climb a mountain. If you're afraid of the water, take swimming lessons. If you're afraid of public speaking, join a Toastmasters club. Doing what you're most afraid of will make you feel less frightened and more capable.

Use visualization. Sports competitors, especially professional athletes and Olympic contenders, use visualization techniques to help them exceed their limitations. Visualization can help you overcome fear by imagining how to cope with fear before it becomes real.

> *My father was my martial arts instructor and I remember that he used to have our group practice meditation. He would have us visualize repeatedly making our moves correctly until we really could perform at our highest level. -Mike*

Take small steps. Fear can feel like an ominous cloud hovering over your life. You can't wipe out years of fear in a day. It will take time and a good strategy to convince your subconscious mind that you're not afraid of whatever is holding you back from experiencing life to the fullest.

Relax. Worrying and fretting about your fears will only exacerbate the emotions involved. Learn how to relax, whether by reading books, taking a class or speaking with a counselor. When you learn how to relax your mind, you'll also learn how to turn your thoughts into less fearful ones.

Take control of your life. Fearful people are usually pessimistic and that powerful force of fear can be like a huge boulder on your back. Fear makes you less likely to break out of a job you hate but more likely to face obstacles that keep you from being truly happy. When you confront your fears and take back control, you'll likely be surprised that the worst you thought could happen doesn't.

If fear in any form is holding you back from developing key skills that could help you reach your ultimate goal in life, you owe it to yourself to explore that fear and take steps to deal with it successfully, once and for all.

LESSONS FROM "FEARLESS" LEADERS

One of the best ways to learn anything is through the experiences of others. There have been extraordinary leaders, entrepreneurs and celebrities who have become over-the-top successes by overcoming odds that you will likely never face. These are people who experienced adversities and trauma throughout their lives but worked to overcome them to reach fabulous heights.

- George Washington, the first President of the United States and a fearless leader during the Revolutionary War, had a serious fear of being buried alive. Actually, his fear may not have been unfounded since medicine was so primitive in those days that people were in danger of being buried alive. But Washington overcame; he didn't let fear deter him as he led his troops into battle against the British.

- TV personality Oprah Winfrey successfully overcame her fear of rejection. She was born in poverty and was told many times that she could never become a television personality because of her looks and her race. She is now one of the world's highest earning entertainers.

- Warren Buffett overcame his insecurities to become one of history's most successful investors. Buffett was especially afraid of public speaking but he soon realized that he would never achieve his dreams unless he could communicate. He enrolled in a Dale Carnegie course that taught him how to get rid of the jitters and is now one of the richest men in the world.

- Emily Dickinson's fear of failure paralyzed her with writer's block. With encouragement and self-analyzing, Dickinson was able to overcome her fear and publish some of the most beautiful poetry ever written.

- Successful women were rare in the days of physicist Marie Curie. She managed to overcome the fear of presenting her ideas to male colleagues and disregarded their jeers and criticism to become an X-ray technology pioneer.

Many other famous and highly successful people were passed over for jobs, failed in athletic pursuits, or suffered major financial loss before they hit the jackpot that took them over the top. If they had let their fears and insecurities rule, they never would have discovered the winning formula.

It's not necessary to expect perfection. You can attempt something and have it fail without losing your drive. There is room for error when you're learning something new, so don't be afraid to fail at those first attempts.

Your fears may seem insurmountable right now, but making a life-changing decision to overcome that which you fear and sticking to a plan can turn your world around. Embrace those challenges and look forward to a successful life on the other side!

APPRECIATE WHO, WHAT AND WHERE YOU ARE

We all have hopes and dreams for the future but every single one of us has made mistakes and we live with regrets. Unfortunately, most people carry the past and the future with them into the present. In short, most of us don't acknowledge where we are right now, today, in this moment.

Your life is a collection of all of your experiences, good and bad. Most people tend to color their future with those experiences. However, sometimes it's best to wipe the slate clean so you can point to a new direction.

For most people this can be a new and potentially confusing concept. Let's take a look at each segment of the idea, starting with appreciating who you are.

WHO ARE YOU?

You are the product of your experiences, knowledge, personality, beliefs and values. You are amazing, unique and wonderful. Yet, like most people, you don't spend much time focusing on your individual greatness.

Rather, your inner voice constantly berates you and points out weaknesses. No wonder it's so difficult to set and keep the right commitments.

STOP!

Action Step #1

Spend some time learning to appreciate "You". Analyze your strengths and weaknesses, so that you can make better decisions going forward.

Who are you? What are you good at? What do you know? How much experience do you have in the areas you're interested in? What makes you special, unique and wonderful? Take some time to write down all of your strengths.

Consider and answer the following:

- Which skills and capabilities do you have?

- In which areas do you excel?

- What would other people consider to be your strengths?

- Which tasks do you find great pleasure in?

Spend some time on this one. Just start writing and, when you get to a point where you can't think of anything else, take a walk and let more ideas come to you.

It's imperative to know what your strengths are so that you can focus your time building them up. They're the building blocks of your commitments and, ultimately, your success.

It's also important to understand your weaknesses. Why? Because knowing and freely admitting your weaknesses motivates you to create stronger support systems and helps you craft lasting commitments.

Your weaknesses don't make you weak and they're nothing to feel bad or guilty about. You're born with talents to capitalize on and weaknesses to manage, overcome or release.

Consider your personal weaknesses and how you think you are viewed by others.

- What are the gaps in your capabilities and skills?

- Which areas do you struggle with or find most frustrating? ?

- What would other people consider to be your weaknesses?

People are frequently conditioned to feel guilty about their weaknesses but, after this exercise, knowing your true strengths will be freeing and energizing.

Some may say that emphasizing and focusing on your strengths is taking the easy way out because they're natural talents, not something you have to work at. However, in the opinion of most successful people, it just makes sense to embrace your innate strengths, skills and talents to develop yourself into what you were made to be.

Do you tell your children to ignore their strengths and focus solely on improving their weaknesses? No, you highlight their strengths and allow them to develop their potential. Why wouldn't you do the same for yourself?

If you're finding this action step difficult, consider using online evaluation tools like the Strengths Finder 2.0, found at www.strengthsfinder.com.

You can take a survey and learn more about your strengths. This information will help you create the commitments that serve you best.

WHAT ARE YOU?

We tend to label ourselves and the labels we use generally aren't positive ones. It's not hard to find people who describe themselves as lazy, fat, dumb or worthless.

More often than not, I've heard people use negative terms to describe themselves. They say, "I'm so stupid." Or "I'm just not good with..."

You name it, I've heard people describe themselves in every negative way possible. If people say to themselves, "I'm so stupid" or "I'm just not good with ___", they are correct. On the other hand, if they say, "I'm so smart" or "I'm good with ___", they're also correct. This is because you believe it to be. I often wonder why it is that we don't use positive terms when we describe ourselves.

What are you? Chances are, once you move past any negative descriptors, you might start listing careers you've had, or your hobbies and pursuits.

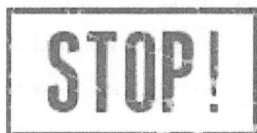

STOP!

Action Step #2

Start making a list of all of the things you are. Stay positive. Are you a vibrant woman with a brilliant mind and a lover of all things creative and artistic?

Are you a fitness enthusiast who enjoys competing? Are you a fan of gadgets and technology who always has the latest and greatest device? What are you and why are you so wonderful?

Again, spend time with this one. Look to your past and the hobbies and interests you once enjoyed, the ones that framed who and what you are now.

WHERE ARE YOU?

Whether you're sitting on your couch watching soap operas or meditating atop a Himalayan mountain, "Where are you" refers to where you are in your life.

Have you achieved your goals? Are you locked into the past or focused on the future? Are you happy with your life right now? What have you accomplished and how has it impacted your life?

Take stock of your life and acknowledge the path you've taken. Appreciate the mistakes you've made and how they've impacted your life.

Appreciate the successes in your life and how they've made you the person you are. Doing this actually frees you from the past. It gives you the power to feel grateful for everything that has occurred in your life, mistakes and challenges included, and to move forward with clarity.

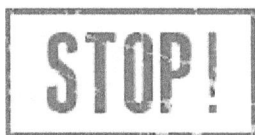

STOP!

Action Step #3

Where are you right now in your life? What are the many things you have that you appreciate? What have you accomplished that you are grateful for? What mistakes have you made that turned you into a better person?

When you write down your thoughts you may realize that, even if you've led a difficult life, everything you've learned has helped put you in a position to create a brilliant and bright future packed with commitment, success and joy.

GRATITUDE IS EVERYTHING

Gratitude is the practice of regularly acknowledging the blessings in your life. When gratitude becomes part of your life, it practically ensures success and joy. When you're grateful for what you have you're better equipped to follow through on your commitments.

Give thanks regularly for what you have, the people in your life, and the simple things that make you smile. You might journal, pray or meditate daily about gratitude.

Gratitude is easier to master when you are able to do the things you love to do. Find something you love and do it often, every day if possible.

Being grateful for what you have puts you in the proper mindset to move forward. To make a commitment that you are motivated by and able to follow through on, you need to know where you're going and what you want. That takes us to the next two action steps.

STOP!

Action Step #4

Create a list of the things that you have the most gratitude for. Come up with a list of at least 50 people, items, beliefs, characteristics, situations and even emotions.

Action Step #5

Consider how you might create a gratitude habit, a daily practice of recognizing everything in your life that you're grateful for.

You might create a daily journal. You might make a mental list during your day. You might share your gratitude via social media. Consider your options and then create whatever gratitude habit feels right for you.

WHERE DO YOU WANT TO BE IN FIVE YEARS?

You've probably been asked that question during a job interview and you may have given an answer that you thought they'd appreciate. However, have you ever really thought about the question for yourself? Consider yourself five years from now. What should your life look like then?

Beth's Story

Beth was a financial advisor. She'd just turned thirty and realized that she didn't really have any plans for the future. When she was asked during her annual job review where she wanted to be in five years, she didn't have an answer.

That moment of anxiety lasted for quite some time. Beth had no idea where her life was going or what she should do. She took some time off and started exploring the possibilities.

She was able to envision herself at 35 and realized that she wanted a management position at her present company. She also wanted to start a family.

Beth returned to her company and asked them to support her schooling for an MBA. They did. She was also able to commit to meeting new people and dating more so she could find a suitable partner and start that family that she wanted.

IF MONEY WERE NO OBJECT

Another way to evaluate what you want is to ask yourself the age-old question, "What would you do if money were no object?" Imagine that you'd won the lottery or come into such a large sum of money that you could do whatever you wanted with your life.

What would you want to do? Many people say that they would travel or buy a place on the coast of some remote Caribbean island. Setting lifestyle aside, what would you DO? How would you spend your days and what would your purpose be?

VOLUNTEER OR BE A SHADOW

If you're unsure exactly what it is that you want (and that's OK), consider identifying and exploring a few possibilities. For example, if you think you might like to get a pet or pursue a career with animals, it might make sense to volunteer at your local animal shelter first.

Or, if you want to improve your financial situation, you might consider shadowing a millionaire or someone who has achieved great financial success. You can learn what you want and don't want when you invest time exploring your options.

SIDE PROJECTS

Have you made a list of the things that you want to do or accomplish? You can call it a task list, bucket list or just side projects. Read, surf the Internet and find other ways to expand on your wish list. Continue exploring these items. As you put your list together, it'll help you identify what you want from life.

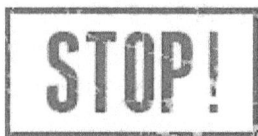

STOP!

Action Step #6

Create a long list of what you want. Which commitments do you want to set and how do you want to change your life? This activity might take some time so give yourself some breathing room to create it. You might need several days to consider what you want from your life.

Charlie's List

Charlie had the task of identifying things that he wanted to do. His list ranges from finishing the kitchen remodel to earning an MBA.

He also wants to learn how to rock climb, save more money for retirement, and do some of his own car repairs. Charlie's list is great because the items came from the heart and are a part of him. They are a positive and proactive combination of his experience and his hopes and dreams for the future.

CREATE YOUR WHY

You now have a list of "what" you want to do. The ideas on the list might range from eating healthier to starting a business. Now comes the next step, the Why. Why do you want to complete the items on your list?

For example, one of the items on Charlie's list was wanting to finish his kitchen remodeling project. Why? Because his wife wanted it done. He wanted it to be finished to make her happy. Great. But his "why" for learning to rock climb was genuine and much more powerful. Charlie was afraid of heights and wanted to overcome that fear in a fun way.

The "why" is essential to your success. If you don't have a strong personal reason to commit to something, it's less likely to happen. You need to dive deeply and discover what is going to motivate you to succeed. The pain of failure should be so great that you'll do anything to make sure you accomplish the task at hand.

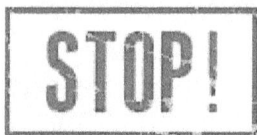

STOP!

Action Step #7

Take a look at your list of "what" items and beside each one, consider your Why. Why do you want to achieve this goal? What's your reasoning and/or motivation?

PURPOSE FOR A COMMITMENT

I have always told folks to develop their purpose and make it as strong as possible; so strong that it makes them cry. Turn your "What" and your "Why" into a purpose statement. A purpose statement is a sentence or two that identifies your goal and your motivation, something that will drive you to stay on track and finish your commitment.

Your purpose statement can and should be personal to you. Some might say something general like, "I will pay off my debt so that I can get a higher credit score."

Well, if a higher credit score is something you take great pride in and you're internally motivated to achieve a particular number, this purpose statement may be fine. However, for most people the desire to pay off debt would have deeper meaning.

They'd aspire to have financial freedom, more discretionary spending money in the future and the ability to save for luxury items, vacations and retirement. So a personal statement that reflected that motivation might look like this:

"I'm tired of living in fear of my debt. I will pay off my debt so that I can live the life I deserve to live. A life that is free from heavy financial burdens and stress. A life where I have the ability to save money for my future."

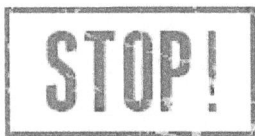

STOP!

Action Step #8

Take a look at your list of goals and your reasons for wanting to achieve them. Practice writing purpose statements for each of them.

As you work through your list, you'll find that some of your items are much more personal than you imagined. You may also uncover more fears and doubts related to those goals.

As these fears and doubts surface, be grateful for them. As you understand yourself better, it will help you create a stronger action plan for your future.

WHY COMMITMENT SETTING IS IMPORTANT

You have a list of goals or commitments. These are things that you want to do or achieve. They vary in intensity and purpose.

Think of at least one major accomplishment in your life that has really made you proud. Now, think of the initial commitment you made when you got started. On a scale of 1-10, how committed were you?

Were you very committed or simply hoping for something good to happen? There's a vast difference between the two. When you simply desire or hope for something, you'll do it only when circumstances make it easy to accomplish.

When you're committed, you accept no excuses, only results. Your commitment becomes part of who you are and every action that you take. Making a commitment, personal or professional, is one of the most fundamental principles of success.

Commitments are powerful because they influence how you think, how you act and how you're perceived. When you make a commitment to yourself, to something or to someone, you're making a promise that is important to you. A promise that you'll do your best to follow through and make it a reality. Your desire to honor your commitment and your promise overpowers your desire to quit.

TOO MANY COMMITMENTS?

It's easy to become committed to too many people, projects and things. Unfortunately, when you overcommit your resources diminish. You run out of time, energy and motivation. It's important to selectively commit. Decide what is truly important to you and commit only to those things.

When you ensure that your commitments are priorities and are important to you, everything improves. Relationships, success and enjoyment all follow commitment.

WILLING TO PAY THE PRICE?

As you work through the purpose statements, you may feel some resistance to particular commitments and begin to scratch some off your list.

For example, perhaps you wrote down that you were committed to going back to school. However, upon writing down your "Why", you realize that the path to going back to school is too steep. It'll take more time than you want to invest and it'll cost more than you can afford.

You need to be willing to pay the price to make and keep a commitment. To be fair, we often don't understand the depth of a commitment until we're in the midst of trying to keep it.

Take marriage, for example. Marriage is a commitment to honor and cherish one person for the rest of your life. No one really understands what that concept means before they get married. They have no idea how the future is going to change each other. They have no idea how long or short "Until death do you part" is actually going to be. You don't know what circumstances could occur to challenge and jeopardize this commitment.

There are unknowns to any commitment you make. Unless you have a crystal ball and can foresee the future, you don't know precisely how easy or difficult it's going to be to keep your commitment.

The point is not to avoid making commitments because of the potential challenges. The point is to make commitments that you're so impassioned by that you don't care what the challenges are—you're going to follow through. Your commitments need to be purposeful and create a positive impact on your life.

BREAKING THROUGH RESISTANCE

What if there are some commitments on your list that appear to be too difficult, too challenging, or perhaps might take too much time to achieve? What do you do with those commitments?

Quite honestly, many of your commitments may frighten you. The depth of the commitment and the energy involved in making them a reality may be quite extensive. It's OK to be frightened. It's OK to feel resistance to your commitments. But, before you scratch them off your list, do this:

Identify why you have resistance. Assess the reality of that resistance. Then imagine what your life would look like A) having achieved the commitment and B) not having achieved the commitment.

Step #1 Identify the Resistance

Why do you encounter resistance to your commitment? Is it because you're afraid of failure? Be honest with yourself. What fears and doubts are you experiencing?

For example, if your commitment is to go back to school to earn a degree and you don't think you have the time to work, tend to your family and attend school, take a look at where those doubts and fears are coming from. Are you really afraid you don't have the time or are you afraid of failing in school?

Step #2 Assess the Validity of the Resistance

Is the resistance really true? Our overly active ego often tells us things that aren't true. It does this to protect us. But, you don't need to be protected from challenges. Life is enriched through experiences and that means taking risks and embracing challenges.

If you're committed to going back to school but experience resistance related to the time commitment, spend a week or two tracking your time.

You can explore methods for saving time in order to free up time to go to school. You just might discover that the "I don't have time" logic is just an excuse and you really do have enough time IF you want to commit to that goal.

Step #3 Imagine Your Life

Take time to daydream. Imagine your life without making a particular commitment. How does your life look and how happy are you?

Now imagine your life after having fulfilled your commitment. How does your life look and how happy are you?

Presumably, having made and fulfilled your commitment means that you're living a better, more joyful and fulfilling life.

Take a look at your list of commitments and purpose statements. Do you feel a positive and excited energy flowing through you? Are you motivated to start making true changes?

It's time to begin harnessing that enthusiasm and fine-tune the commitments you make and the direction your life will take.

STOP!

Action Step #9

Get excited! Imagine who or what you will become. Envision the possibilities of your commitments. How will they impact your life?

How will your life change as a result of honoring your commitments?

Imagine the inner strength, peace and confidence you'll gain from becoming a person who sets meaningful goals and follows through on those goals.

Begin creating your future right now. As you imagine becoming a commitment keeper you begin to become that person. Your vision becomes your reality.

Action Step #10

Become aware of your ability to persist and persevere. Write down the goals and commitments that you have honored. When did your commitments mean something to you? What were they and what did they mean? How did honoring those commitments change you and change your life? This is an important exercise. Don't skip it. It will help you fully grasp the concept of the power of commitments.

It will help build confidence in yourself and in the commitments and promises you make. You'll begin to erase fear and doubt and replace it with faith and confidence in yourself and in the world around you.

You now have what you need to take the next step and actually begin to make those deep and profound commitments to yourself and to others.

Excited? Let's move forward with confidence!

6

I'VE BEEN WORKING FOR THE RAILROAD

"Man, alone, has the power to transform his thoughts into physical reality; man, alone, can dream and make his dreams come true.
— *Napoleon Hill*

VISION OF THE FUTURE

Several years ago on an extremely hot day, a crew was working on the roadbed of the railroad when they were interrupted by a slow moving train. The train ground to a stop and a window in the air conditioned last car was raised.

A booming, friendly voice called out, "Dave, is that you?" Dave Anderson, the crew chief called back, "Sure is, Jim, and it's really good to see you." With that pleasant exchange, Dave Anderson was invited to join Jim Murphy, the president of the railroad, for a visit. For more than an hour the men exchanged pleasantries and then shook hands warmly as the train pulled out.

Dave Anderson's crew immediately surrounded him and a man expressed astonishment that he knew Jim Murphy as a personal friend. Dave then explained that 23 years earlier he and Jim began work on the same day. One of the men, half jokingly and half seriously, asked Dave why he was still working out in the hot sun while Jim Murphy was now company president.

Rather wistfully Dave explained, "Twenty-three years ago I went to work *ON* the railroad while Jim Murphy went to work *FOR* the railroad."

TIME FOR ACTION

It's time to take action. It's time to turn that list of wants, whys and purpose statements into a prioritized list of commitments.

I strongly recommend focusing on one priority commitment at a time. Let that commitment become ingrained in your life and a part of who you are.

The ultimate goal is to create a pattern of success and follow-through. Make it a habit to carefully evaluate and assess your life, goals, wants and needs before you make a new commitment.

STOP!

Action Step #1

What's most important to you right now and will it make the biggest impact on your life? Review your list of wants and contemplate what you want to achieve.

You may have many goals, ideas and commitments that you want to make. Consider the impact that each will have on your life.

A commitment to get a degree may have much broader reaching results than a commitment to save money for a house or to spend more time with your friends.

Evaluate your commitments and identify the ones that have the potential to change your life in a major way. Focus on these for now.

Aim Past Your Target

I was trained in the martial arts from a very early age and one of the things I remember most was when the instructor (who was my Dad, by the way) taught us to break boards and bricks with bare hands, feet, or even our head. He used to stress that, when you see the target in front of you, don't focus on hitting the target. Focus on hitting beyond it so that you burst or drive through the object.

A dream or goal is no different. No matter what you're aiming for, make sure to see yourself bursting beyond the object of your commitment. See yourself driving through it.

One thing to remember about goals is that you may not accomplish them according to your time schedule. That's OK. Of course, you want to accomplish the goal but life throws curves at us all the time. If it was easy everyone could do it. Before you can feel the joy of accomplishing your goal, you will be tested. But you'll know what it took to get to the finish line and be able to share that testimony. The destination is not the true success. The journey and who you become on the way marks the true success. Continue to reorganize and adjust.

Astronauts know that they are off course 99% of the time so they must constantly adjust to be able to accomplish their mission. You're no different as you make adjustments on your path to accomplish what you committed to.

Now it's time to unlock the potential of this commitment. Keep in mind that following through on your commitments will change your life, make you a better person and lead to future successful commitments.

DO YOU HAVE WHAT YOU WANT?

Why is getting what you want in life so difficult? Is it because you are lazy or that your desire just isn't strong enough? Or, maybe your priorities aren't in order? There's an endless supply of excuses to choose from.

Form a brand new habit by developing stronger willpower. When you start a new habit it takes approximately three weeks until it is formed in your brain. At the three week mark you begin to act automatically.

Developing your willpower will help you overcome obstacles and lead to wise decisions. You will be less likely to make spur of the moment choices or take actions that could have devastating consequences.

EXAMINE YOUR ROUTINE

Look at your daily routine. What consumes most of your time? Try to identify where you feel overloaded.

Maybe it's watching too much television, spending too much time on Facebook, or subscribing to too many blogs and newsletters. Perhaps you're just glued to your cell phone. Calculate how many hours you spend on such activities and cut them in half.

After a week, look at your results. Did you do better than before you were tracking your time? More importantly, did you have more time for what you really wanted to do?

BREAKING THOSE HABITS

Who doesn't have habits that they want to break? Many of us may have wanted to lose a few pounds, give up smoking or just become more assertive.

Breaking any habit involves using your willpower, self-discipline and self-control. These skills are important and can make a huge difference when it comes to personal growth.

If you demonstrate these skills you're often viewed as a proactive person; those who are lacking are viewed as lazy. Remember, it's possible to learn how to develop and improve these skills.

The best way to overcome the feeling that you are unmotivated or lazy is to start doing things. This includes performing tasks that make you feel uncomfortable.

If you are feeling shy about something, take small steps to overcome it. Once you start forcing yourself to take action you will find that your negative inner voice starts to quiet. You will begin developing a positive inner voice which compels you to take action.

Finding your focus will enable you to strengthen your willpower. One way to accomplish this is by removing as many distractions as possible. If you take a quick look around you, you will notice that many people have music playing or are chatting on the phone or sending text messages. These things distract your focus.

If you are at work and feel distracted, try using earphones to muffle the distractions. Other things you can do to minimize distractions include simply shutting your door, finding a quiet place to work, turning off your phone's ringer, ignoring your email and logging off from social sites. By implementing these changes you'll find that the task gets finished quickly and you'll feel less drained.

People tend to focus more on breaking a habit versus building or forming a new one. It's human nature to perceive something new as a challenge. Your mind automatically starts thinking negatively about the prospect of doing anything new so, when it comes to forming a new habit, take things slowly and set mini goals. Instead of telling yourself that you'll exercise for 30 minutes, get up early and aim for five minutes instead. Slowly increase the amount of time until you're at the 30 minute level. By the time you reach this milestone you'll be well on your way to instilling a habit.

Darren Hardy discusses this principle in his book, "The Compound Effect". He talks about taking small steps each day then slowly increasing over time. The simple disciplines done repeatedly will lead to your success. For example, if you want to quit caffeine don't go cold turkey. Drink one cup of coffee a day, then go to one every two days until you reach a point where you're drinking caffeine only once a month and eventually not at all.

> *Make it enjoyable.* Exercise might be far more enjoyable if you join a basketball league instead of running on a lonely treadmill. Working on the computer might be a lot easier out on your deck with the birds and the trees in the background.

> *Focus on your motivation.* Why is this goal relevant to you? Imagine how it will feel to accomplish it. Self-motivation is often the only way to get yourself to do something you don't want to do.

> *Stay in the present.* We're great at making ourselves feel bad about things that either happened in the past or haven't happened yet. Avoid thinking about the unpleasant activity until it's time.

THE BENEFITS OF WILLPOWER

The biggest benefit of developing willpower is inner strength. You will have the ability to take action when necessary and be able to stay on task and follow through.

You may find that you have more energy and drive and this spreads to those around you. How many times have you met with people who are emotional and after spending time with them you developed the same mood?

This is why it's important to connect with people who have a similar mindset. A well-known study suggests that the five people you spend the most time with are who you become. So, if you spend time with negative, poor, or moody people, guess what rubs off on you? Align yourself with those who have a common goal.

Increasing your willpower leads to better concentration and more control of your entire lifestyle.

IDENTIFYING CHOICES AND TAKING ACTION

It's common for people to make impulsive decisions and then not acknowledge responsibility for their actions. Kids use this excuse all the time. "I don't know why, I just did!"

This is not the proper attitude. Instead, force yourself to become aware of what you are thinking and what consequence each action will have. Every action has a reaction. What you do today will determine what happens tomorrow.

Suppose you want to start a new exercise program. Why do you really want to exercise? Is it to look good or to show your children that exercise is healthy?

Teaching your children to be healthy would be the obvious choice but your real reason could be because you want to look great in that new Armani suit! This is your real reason and the one that compels you to take consistent action.

REFUSE TO BE LAZY

By refusing to become a lazy person you are taking a step in the right direction. It's so easy to just not do something and let an opportunity slip by. It's much harder to take decisive action but the results can be rewarding.

Refusing to be lazy takes work. Your first step is to not let your inner voice talk you out of doing something. Instead, take action no matter how small it may be.

A great example of this occurs when you get home from work. You may feel like just grabbing some fast food and watching mindless TV; instead, try going for a walk or cooking a healthy dinner.

PUSHING YOURSELF TO OVERCOME CHALLENGES

You should be careful not to make emotional decisions because your desire to do the task typically fades quickly.

A perfect example of this is when you make a New Year's resolution. These resolutions are often emotional, based on certain things you were thinking about at the time. They are often not well thought out or planned.

On the other hand, by pushing yourself you are ultimately building willpower. This training takes time and effort but also develops your concentration levels, self-confidence and assertiveness.

You may have decided that you're going to get up earlier each morning and go for a walk or get on your treadmill. Before you go to bed you set your alarm clock for 5:00 am. The buzzer goes off and even though you may hit the snooze button, you have set another alarm for 5:05 am. This second alarm is your 'pushing' mechanism.

You feel great once you've exercised. You feel energized and ready to face the day. Capture this feeling and remember it, then use it tomorrow when deciding whether to hit snooze or get up.

Can you see that by planning ahead you can create something which will 'push' you to take action? Develop a habit of training yourself and your mind to become stronger.

COMPLETE TASKS ON TIME

You can challenge yourself to start completing tasks on time. Think of a small task that needs to be done around your home. It could be cleaning a room or organizing your desk.

Once you've decided on your task, choose a time to do it and write it down. Set a reminder on your phone or write it on your calendar. When the time comes, make sure you actually do your task.

If the task is large, set a time limit and work until your time is up. Use an alarm clock to remind you of the time. Once that buzzer goes off, take a rest and congratulate yourself for completing the task. If you're feeling energized you can continue and complete the task; otherwise schedule another time to complete it.

I have developed a great tool that helps us stick to our plans each day; a one-page form called "Daily Commitment Productivity Planner Sheet". At the end of the day I sit down and make a list of the people I need to call the next day, no matter what. I also list the emails that must be sent out, no matter what.

After I determine our top three daily commitments, we write the five major things I need to do to move those commitments along. I then identify the people I need to reach out to that day, no matter what, to help us move our commitments forward. Finally, I make a list of people were waiting to hear from to help move our commitment forward.

I will also outline our early-morning, mid-morning, mid-day and evening schedules. All my daily routines are included: reading my emails in the morning (once a day), 15 minutes of personal development and prayer, meditation, food and workout plans, ways to improve my relationships and scheduled events for the kids.

When I wake up each morning I already have an outline for the day and a complete plan of what needs to get done. I understand that sometimes things come up and your schedule needs to change. But, if this happens, at least you have already set a clear direction, which allows you to adjust accordingly.

You can download a copy of the Commitment Productivity Planner at

www.ManagingYourCommitmentToSuccess.com/downloads

DAILY COMMITMENT PRODUCTIVITY PLANNER SHEET

Date: _____ M Tu W Th F Sa Su

Commitment #1:

Commitment #2:

Commitment #3:

PRIORITIES

DAILY ROUTINE
Early Morning
Mid Morning
Afternoon
Evening

NOTES:

YOUR PLAN OF DAC

DAC is a simple reminder tool. It stands for *Decisions*, *Actions* and *Consequences*.

> *Decisions* – You must decide that you wish to make a change. No matter what it is, a firm decision must be made.
>
> *Actions* – Write down an idea, make a call or talk to people about your idea. Until you take action nothing will happen.
>
> *Consequences* – How will your actions affect your life? Is going out for a few beers a good idea or will it cloud your judgment? Will not making that call today result in lost opportunity?

Every choice we make causes change. Temptation is the one thing that can easily destroy your plans. If you have a plan of DAC in place you will be equipped with powerful tools.

Let's take your food choices as an example. Every Friday someone brings donuts to work and you're always tempted to have one. Instead of giving in, activate your DAC plan. It's easy to take a healthier choice to work with you; this could be a whole grain muffin or a piece of fruit and yogurt.

When it's time for your morning break you already have your snack with you. You won't be tempted to reach for that donut.

Another way to stay in control of your eating habits is by preparing easy meals in advance. By planning your weekly menu you won't have to think about your food choices.

By deciding in advance how you're going to react to certain situations you remain in control of the choices you make. If you know you're going out to a buffet dinner tell yourself ahead of time what you're going to eat.

HOW EXERCISE CAN INCREASE YOUR WILLPOWER

When it comes to losing weight or sticking with an exercise program, your willpower often gets credit for your results, good or bad. Set small goals that are achievable and specific. Instead of saying, "I will lose 20 pounds by August", it's much better to tell yourself, "I will cut out 300 calories today." By doing something which is immediate you'll be in control and able to attain your goal quickly.

Guilt is an emotion which is directly attached to your willpower. It's so easy to miss a workout and then spend the rest of the day feeling guilty about it. If this happens regularly why not exercise with a partner? When you know you have to meet a friend, you're less likely to let them down. Your guilty conscience will nag at you when you're tempted to miss your workout appointment.

LEAVE WORK AT WORK

One of the main drains on willpower in today's world is stress. If your job is stressful, make a point of walking during your lunch hour. By getting out of the office and experiencing a change of scenery you can easily recharge your batteries. This will help you feel refreshed and energetic enough to deal with the afternoon rush.

An important rule to follow is this: once you've finished work for the day, make a point of not thinking about it at home. This is really difficult for many people but enjoying your free time will truly help decrease your stress level.

HOW TO INCREASE YOUR WILLPOWER

Imagine how your life would be if you could accomplish your tasks without procrastinating. People we consider successful are simply able to get themselves to do things the rest of us don't like to do. Self-discipline is the key ingredient to reaching the highest level of success in your life. Spend a few minutes every day learning how to train your willpower and view it as a muscle that needs to be strengthened. Be specific.

Whether you're working toward a career goal or finishing a project at home, be sure what you want to do.

The words you use are important here. The statement, "I will" shows much more self-discipline than, "I'll try." Set yourself up for success with a firm decision to accomplish your goal.

Self-discipline requires a certain degree of focus. What you plan to do or want to do must be so important that it stays in the forefront of your mind until you achieve it. Leave a sticky note on the bathroom mirror or computer screen so you can remember what you're doing.

Record milestones, both projected and achieved. Keep track of the tasks and projects that contribute to your goals and celebrate your achievements along the way.

Hang out with people you admire. One of the best ways to learn how to improve in one area of your life is to gravitate towards people who do well in that area. Make friends with people you admire for their self-discipline, follow-through and ability to accomplish goals.

Apply your keen observation skills to see how they do it; ask questions. Compliment them, let yourself be inspired by people who are living their dreams.

Increasing your self-discipline is definitely possible, but results will not come overnight. Put your emotion into the process, not the end result. Don't allow yourself to worry about money, relationships, possessions, clothing or food. Let your mind be free to focus on the goal at hand. Plan your tasks when you're not likely to be distracted by other interesting or enjoyable activities.

Self-discipline is like anything else—with practice, it becomes a positive habit. Self-discipline is developed one decision at time and gets a little easier each time.

Most importantly, acknowledge the times you are successful in showing self-discipline. Any behavior that is rewarded is more likely to reappear.

HOW DOES FOLLOWING THROUGH BENEFIT YOU?

Following through on your intentions, promises and goals makes a world of difference. It's a powerful thing, actually. Even the simple process of following through on household chores can change your life.

You pay more attention to the things you do. When you focus your attention on the tasks at hand you do a better job and spend much less time re-doing them. You spend less time apologizing for mistakes because projects get done right the first time.

When you give your full attention to a project or task, you're able to be "in the moment". There's joy in that process, even when you're doing something as mundane as a household chore.

REMOVE YOUR ROADBLOCKS

Simply setting the right intention and establishing commitments that are true to who you are and where you want to go helps identify your potential roadblocks. It also helps establish the passion and motivation required to achieve success.

Putting 100% of yourself into a task or project and becoming as productive as possible is key. If your attention isn't divided you'll accomplish so much more.

You'll also be able to more readily identify what is important to you and why it's important. When you're able to pursue goals and commitments with certainty, you remove roadblocks.

When you want something badly enough you'll kick down doors to make it happen. That's when you know you've set the best intention and established a commitment that you can follow through on. You'll be willing to do whatever it takes to make it happen.

TAKE CHARGE OF YOUR LIFE

You appreciate everything more when you're able to put your whole self into your tasks, actions and responsibilities. You'll feel more satisfaction, pride and confidence. You'll actually feel more in control of your life.

You'll even experience better mental health. You'll go to bed knowing that, regardless of how the day's events turned out, you did your best.

STOP!

Action Step #2

Identify the commitment that you're going to set first and create a Mission Statement around that commitment. You can fill in the blanks to get started:

"I am a committed _____ (or I am committed to _____). I will do everything in my power to ensure that _____. This means _____.

To attain my commitment and to honor my promise, I will _____ so that I can _____.

I will continue to _____ so that I can _____."

You now have the foundation for honoring your commitment. You know your "What" and "Why". You've identified your priority commitment and know the purpose behind your commitment. But something's still missing.

Now you need a plan to make your commitment an integral part of your life. In the next chapter, we'll teach you how to follow through and honor your commitment and, by doing that, bring lasting **Passion**, **Purpose** and **Success**.

7

HOW TO MAKE A D.R.I.V.E COMMITMENT

"Productivity is never an accident. It is always the result of a commitment to excellence, intelligent planning and focused effort."
— Paul J. Meyer

DON'T HOLD BACK

Take a certain goal of yours and double it, or triple it. Or, multiply it by 10. Then ask yourself what you would have to do to achieve that new goal. I used this strategy recently with a salesman friend of mine. He said he was selling $100,000 worth of product each month but wanted to get to $140,000.

I asked him to tell me what it would take for him to sell $200,000 worth of equipment each month. "$200,000!" he shouted. "That's impossible. I'm leading the team already with $100,000, and nobody thought that could be done."

"What would you have to do?" I persisted. "If your life depended on hitting $200,000 next month, what exactly would you do?"

He laughed and then started listing things as I wrote them down on a note pad. "I'd have to be two places at once," he said. "I'd have to make twice as many presentations as I'm making. I'd have to present to two clients at once!"

Then it hit him. All of a sudden he got the idea that he might be able to stage a large presentation of his product with a number of clients in the room at one time. "I could rent a room at a hotel and have 20 people in for coffee and donuts and I could make a big deal out of it," he said.

A number of other ideas came to him; combining his cold-calling with his travel time, utilizing e-mail as a sales tool, using his administrative staff better. Idea after idea came to him while I wrote furiously on the pad. All of the ideas were a result of his thinking big. He reached sales of $200,000 the very next month!

If you have enjoyed any success, you're probably no stranger to goal setting. In order to get anywhere in life, we must have a vision of where we want to be. We must take the time to think about exactly what we want to do instead of merely jumping at any opportunity that comes our way.

Admittedly, the act of setting goals doesn't guarantee success. But when done properly, it does provide a target to shoot for.

DO YOU HAVE THE D.R.I.V.E.?

Anyone who's been in the corporate world has heard about S.M.A.R.T. goals: Specific, Measurable, Attainable, Realistic and Time-bound. That works pretty well for people who produce spreadsheets and checklists but it doesn't work as well for those who want to capture the entrepreneurial spirit.

High-performance author and trainer Brendon Burchard points out that we have become a work culture that sets its goals too small. Where are the moon shot dreams these days? Was it a S.M.A.R.T. goal for Columbus to sail across the ocean or for Martin Luther King to march on Washington? Was it a S.M.A.R.T. goal for Jonas Salk to experiment for a polio vaccine? Steve Jobs didn't create Apple to make PC clones did he?

Those were impossible dreams and we have to rekindle those to make our economy vibrant again. Let's get away from using the acronym S.M.A.R.T. and develop a new one called **D.R.I.V.E.**

The D stands for Dream. Bill and Melinda Gates are using their billions to help eradicate malaria around the world. That, folks, is not a realistic dream. But that's the kind of thinking that will eventually lead to a cure. Look back a few decades to the U.S. space program. We had no idea how to get to the moon when President John F. Kennedy promised that we'd land a man there by the end of the decade. Our greatest scientific minds had to scramble to invent the tools and technology to get our astronauts there and back safely. Neil Armstrong and Buzz Aldrin took the first steps on the moon on July 20, 1969 and the positive results of the space program are still pouring in.

The R stands for Reach. Airbnb will soon overtake all the big names as the world's largest hotel chain and they don't even own a single hotel. Airbnb, which allows users to rent out their spare rooms or vacant homes to strangers, surpassed 10 million stays in 2013 and tripled revenue. They went to market with a huge goal to reach the worldwide market as soon as possible but have been more successful than even their most optimistic estimates. Don't be afraid to set your goals extremely high.

The I stands for Inspiration. When we are inspired, we are in Spirit. We work well in this state because inspiration gives us boundless energy to pursue what we're best at doing. It could be a new idea for a home appliance or a solar powered device for impoverished countries.

Inspired people don't take no for an answer and often produce new, more efficient ways to accomplish their goals.

The V stands for Vision. Sometimes an entrepreneur has a vivid, imaginative concept that sounds so far-fetched everyone else thinks he's gone mad. Who would've thought that Amazon would break the barrier from being just a bookseller to now operating one of the premier delivery platforms in the world? Jeff Bezos has vision and his company reaps billions of dollars each year because he foresaw the ability to expedite just about anything under the sun. Exercise your vision and see the possibilities that lie ahead.

The E stands for Execution. Nothing gets done and nobody gets paid unless you execute the plan. Aside from the initial idea, this is the most important stage. Build a team that can develop a strong gameplan, then use sound business practices to take your idea to the top. Look at Google and see how the $350 billion behemoth is still agile enough to enter new markets. Sure, they purchase a lot of the leading edge technology but they execute well while their competition struggles to keep pace.

AVOID VAGUENESS – BE SPECIFIC

Many of us have goals that are just too vague. Some people make commitments to:

- Save money

- Eat healthier

- Start a business

While making these commitments may be better than nothing, they are far too ambiguous. If you want to save money, you can accomplish that by saving an extra $1 this year. But is that the kind of progress you really want to make?

Saving more money than last year is a little better. It at least gives you a semblance of a goal to work with because you have your figures from last year to compare. But again, if you save $1 more than you did last year, you've technically achieved your goal.

In order for commitments to be the most effective, they must be concrete. Instead of setting a commitment to save money or to save more than last year, identify a percentage or dollar figure to aim for. This will help motivate you and give you a benchmark to measure your achievements.

Remember, a goal is just a timeline for finishing something you want.

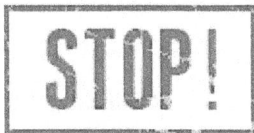

STOP!

Action Step #1

Take one of your commitments and make it clearly identifiable and measureable.

Action Step #2

Make your commitments part of your daily conversation. Make positive statements that affirm their achievement.

Action Step #3

Get excited by the "Why". Define your commitment in terms that excite all your senses.

SET TIME LIMITS

In order for a commitment to be effective, it's best to set a time limit for it. Do you want to achieve success in one year, in ten years, or by next month?

Indefinite commitments have a way of setting us up for procrastination and failure. If we run across an obstacle, we're more inclined to put the commitments off until a more convenient time. Quite often, we keep putting them off until we either lose hope or forget about them entirely.

A commitment with a time limit puts us under pressure. We may not like the sound of that, but it's actually a good thing. If you make a promise that must be met within a certain time frame, you are more likely to work as hard as necessary to achieve it by the deadline. You establish a commitment that must be honored.

STOP!

Action Step #4

Establish a deadline for your commitment. When will you have achieved success and followed through on your promise? It doesn't matter if it's a long or short-term commitment; decide when you want to celebrate success and set a deadline.

Remember, to stay on course it's important to have both short-term and long-term steps toward your commitment. The short-term ones give us smaller victories that keep us motivated and the long-term commitments ensure that we have something to work toward.

Each long-term step should be broken down into smaller short-term promises. For example, you might want to make $1 million in sales this year. That's a good goal but it's hard to monitor your progress.

Instead, figure out how much you'll need to sell each month. One million dollars divided by 12 gives you a monthly goal of $83,333.

This technique can also help you determine whether or not a commitment is attainable. For instance, if you're looking to save $1 million for retirement, you know that you have a certain number of years to accomplish it.

If you don't have the income to attain that level of savings, you can create plans to achieve your goal by reducing expenses or creating some type of additional income.

STOP!

Action Step #5

Make your commitments BIG enough to stretch your abilities. Break through that board! Know your limits, but never stop trying to exceed them.

Action Step #6

See your commitments daily. Close your eyes and see yourself achieving your commitment with absolute clarity.

Action Step #7

Act as if you already achieved your commitments. Take actions and make plans as if you've already reached your goal

Action Step #8

Socialize your commitments. Associate with like-minded people. Avoid the nay-sayers. Mastermind and discuss your commitments and share your ideas with people who are interested in achieving similar goals.

PUT YOUR GOALS IN WRITING

One of the most important steps when establishing commitments is to write them down. It sounds very basic, but you'd be surprised at how many people fail to do this.

If you make promises but don't write them down, it's harder to stick to them. They might be in the back of your mind but they're not staring you in the face. Writing your commitments down in a conspicuous place forces you to revisit them from time to time, providing motivation and a sense of accountability.

In addition to writing down your commitments, try writing notes about your progress in your success journal. This will give you insight into what you might have done differently to achieve a better outcome and aid in future commitments and planning. Remember, it's important to be flexible and to regularly assess your progress.

In an effort to help you stay on track and positive we're going to take a look at affirmations and power statements.

They will help you change your outlook and help give you the mindset you need to persevere and stay positive.

WHAT ARE AFFIRMATIONS?

Affirmations are wonderfully positive statements that help turn your negative thoughts, limiting beliefs, and unproductive or unhealthy habits into positive thoughts and actions.

The power of positive thinking has been studied by the psychiatric, medical, scientific and spiritual communities. They've all determined the same thing; positive thinking has tremendous power.

Affirmations play a critical role in modifying your thinking. They help you not only to embrace success but also to expect it. A positive affirmation is a statement you can use to replace a commonly held negative statement. For example:

"I'll never be accepted into business school." – Negative statement/belief

"I am worthy of success and have the skills, the knowledge and perseverance to achieve my MBA." – Positive affirmation

HOW DO AFFIRMATIONS WORK?

One of the most difficult challenges we face is dealing with the six inches between our ears. Changing your mindset is the single most powerful step you can take to change your life. Henry Ford wrote these words many years ago but they are still very true today.

"What you believe, you manifest and attract".

The thoughts you put into your head are very important. If you put negative beliefs into your head you can become negative.

When you're in a negative state of mind, you expect negative things to happen. You don't expect to succeed or to be able to honor your commitments. Your thoughts become your reality. If you think you'll never meet your goals, that is exactly what you will experience.

You are your harshest critic. Chances are you spend your days thinking negative thoughts and buying into limiting beliefs that you're not even aware of. For example:

- I'm never going to have enough money

- I'll never be able to make this work

- I'll always be stuck in this crappy job

On and on it goes all day long, every single day. It doesn't have to be this way. If you change your thoughts through an affirmation habit and begin to think and believe, "I am worthy and skilled and the right lifestyle is waiting for me," your thoughts will soon become your reality.

That's where positive affirmations become a very useful tool.

Changing your mindset changes your reality and your results. When you replace your negative thoughts and limiting beliefs with a positive affirmation, the negativity disappears like dust in the wind.

You can then focus on productive and healthy thoughts that support you as you follow through on your commitments.

The key, of course, is to create affirmations that help you to succeed and train you to expect success. With the right affirmation habit, your mind, body and soul respond and your life will transform. Positive affirmations help you change your thinking by giving you something to lean on. They help you stay aware of your thoughts, the first step to changing them.

TIPS FOR BETTER AFFIRMATIONS

1. Write them using active and present language. Say "I am" not "I will be."

2. Use the word "I". Make yourself part of the affirmation.

3. Be Positive. Use words that make you feel motivated and excited. Embrace powerful language
and find words that resonate with you.

"All My Relationships Are Loving
And Harmonious."

"I Choose To Make Positive Healthy Choices
For Myself."

"I Know I Deserve Success and Accept
It Now."

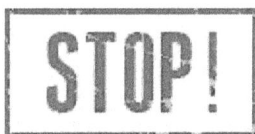

STOP!

Action Step #4

Write affirmations for yourself. Explore some of
your limiting beliefs and the negative thoughts
that creep into your mind.

Write an affirmation for each of those negative
thoughts or limiting beliefs. Work on each affirmation until you create one that resonates with you.

Self-created affirmations are much more powerful
but I understand if you need some help getting
the creative juices flowing. What's important is
that you start replacing negative thoughts with
positive ones.

Take a look at the wording in your affirmations. Keep working until each affirmation makes you feel excited and motivated.

Action Step #5

Develop an affirmation habit, something that you will do every day, perhaps several times each day. You want to have your affirmation ready to go so you can quickly wipe away the negative thoughts and replace them with positive ones.

Now there is no right or wrong way to create an affirmation habit. However, the habit must meet your needs and personality.

There are many ways to embrace your affirmation habit. It's OK to get creative and find a system that works for you.

1. **Meditation**—If you meditate, replace your mantra with your affirmation.

2. **Visual Cues**—If you're a visual person, print out your affirmations and place them in a location where you'll see them often. Hang them on your mirror or over your desk.

3. **Audible Cues**—Record your affirmations on a voice recorder and listen to them as part of your morning routine.

4. **Write Them Down**—If you're a writer or you enjoy journaling, write your affirmations several times per day.

I recently learned about someone who uses the scheduling software on their phone to send themselves multiple affirmations via text message.

In my book "Mastering of The Mindset - The Power of Affirmations", I teach you more in-depth how to develop affirmations with a 33-day exercise. You can learn more by visiting www.MasteringOfTheMindset.com

BE PATIENT WITH YOURSELF

Every master was once a disaster before they became a master at what they do. Don't focus on perfect efforts and results; enjoy your efforts. If you're consistently taking positive steps, you're on the path to living your ideal life.

8

KEEP DIGGING! YOU'RE ALMOST THERE!

Unless commitment is made, there are only
promises and hopes...but no plans.
—*Peter Drucker*

THREE MORE FEET

During the California gold rush two brothers sold all they had and went prospecting. They discovered a vein they thought would pay off, staked a claim, and got down to digging.

Everything seemed to be going well, but then the vein of gold disappeared! The brothers continued to pick away for a while, with no success. Finally, they threw in the shovel.

They sold their equipment and claim rights for a few hundred dollars and returned home. The man who bought the claim hired an engineer who advised him to continue digging in the same spot where the brothers had left off.

Sure enough, three feet deeper, the new owner struck gold. A little more persistence and the brothers would've been millionaires! There is gold in you, too. How much further do you need to dig?

CREATE YOUR OWN FUTURE

We've taken a look at who you are, including your strengths and weaknesses. We've taken a look at where you are right now, as well as where you want to be. You've identified commitments you want to make and dig deep to identify the purpose and the "Why" for each of those commitments. Now it's time to create your future. It's time to figure out all of the steps you need to take to go from where you are right now to where you want to be.

CREATE A PLAN OF ACTION

An action plan is much more detailed than you might imagine, but it's also quite invigorating to create. This is when you begin to realize not only what's possible but also how dramatically your life is going to change. Your action plan will contain the following:

Your long term goal

What are you committing to? Are you committing to starting a business? Going back to school? Re-invigorating your marriage? Obtaining a promotion? Traveling overseas? Saving more for retirement?

What exactly are you committing to? If possible, identify the commitment in measurable terms.

For example, "I am going to launch my business in January 2016." Or "I am going to save an additional 10% of my income toward retirement."

Short Term Goals

What steps do you need to take to make your commitment a reality? For example, if you're committing to becoming an executive, what do you need to do to achieve it?

If you're committing to saving more for retirement, what steps must you take to achieve your goal?

Resources

Identify your resources. Resources include people, technology, systems, time and finances.

Timeline

If you're committed to saving for retirement and your first steps are to cancel cable and trade in your car, when will you have those goals accomplished?

Armed with your goals, resources and timeline, it's now time to create an action plan.

STOP!

Action Step #1

Create your action plan. You can structure it however, you want but it's important to have it documented.

You might find that a checklist works for you or that a spreadsheet or a written document works better. Some people find that a printed checklist placed in the middle of their desk works best. Others prefer digital calendars and daily reminders.

I use small paper calendars and break them apart. I figure out how long it should take to achieve my commitment and work backwards to fill in the steps to achieve it. I break it into small goals with target dates. Once I have dates and timelines I paste the calendars on the wall so I can see them every day to keep me on track.

No matter which system you choose, make sure it's one that you can and will follow.

ONE SMALL STEP CAN CHANGE YOUR LIFE

Invisible Hours

Many people think that Michael Phelps is a freak of nature. The truth is, he was not born to be a swimming superstar. It was a skill he developed over many years. He committed time, energy and persistence to turn himself into an Olympic champion.

Phelps had a dream to win Olympic gold and he would train feverishly to fulfill the dream. He would begin his daily training hours before his competition. Those "invisible hours" often resulted in that precious millisecond between victory and second place. This is what separates the legends from the forgotten ones.

Who among us is willing to sacrifice what Michael Phelps has sacrificed? He has paid the price many times over and earned the global respect that he deserves by committing to every task it took to achieve greatness.

What are YOU doing to stand out, to go that extra mile? How many invisible hours are you putting in to achieve greatness? Are you just kicking the tires or are you running at your highest level of performance? You must work for it, claw for it, despite all the odds or obstacles.

Commit with all your heart and ability. Focus every bit of your talent on achieving your goals or commitments. Remember that great achievements demand great sacrifices. Pay your dues and put in the invisible hours; don't coast and never put your life on auto-pilot.

Creating your action plan can be an exciting and invigorating experience. You're able to track what you need to do to change your life. You'll be able to envision what your life will look like and the process needed to get there.

However, it's all still fiction until you take that first step. The first step, whatever it may be, can be terrifying. It means that you are actually committing to what you've only thought and written about. Action follows commitment and deep intention.

On the day when you take the first step of your action plan here's what I want you to do – celebrate!

Do something joyous for yourself.

Plan it in advance so that you have the time and means to follow through. For example, if you commit to going back to school, and your first step is to apply to colleges, take time to celebrate the accomplishment when you send your first application.

Go for a hike, buy school supplies or go have lunch with a friend. Just do something for yourself that makes you smile and acknowledges the fact that you've taken a positive step toward a commitment.

DEVELOP A VISION

Close your eyes and imagine what your life will look like when you've honored your commitment. How will your life change throughout the process? What positive elements of the change can you focus on so that your vision is one that is optimistic and powerful?

If your goal is to save more money, that likely means giving up things that you currently enjoy. How can you make that financial sacrifice something that is positive?

Going back to school or starting a business involves a time commitment as well as stepping into an unfamiliar environment. How can you turn those into positive changes? Create a vision for yourself that focuses on the constructive and encouraging aspects of change.

CLARIFY YOUR VALUES

Values are a person's principles or standards of behavior. Remembering and clarifying your values will help you create a solid and optimistic vision.

Most of us don't spend much time thinking about this. It involves considering how important the following values, and others, are:

- Spiritual belief

- Wealth

- Social connections

- Social power and influence

- Politeness

- Creativity

- Family

- Patriotism

Understanding what is important to you will help you create a sustainable vision that supports your success.

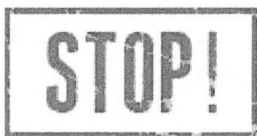

STOP!

Action Step #2

Make a list of your values and prioritize them. Learn, discover and remember what's important to you and why you're establishing the commitments that you're going to follow through on. Why do they matter and how do they reflect or support your values?

KEEPING YOUR BALANCE

While everyone should live a balanced life, yours may look quite different from that of others. Review your priorities and what makes you happy and fulfilled. Some people may prioritize self-care over social status. If so, their values and lifestyle will be different.

Identify what a balanced life means to you and recognize signs of imbalance:

- Sadness or Depression

- Fatigue

- Anger

- Frustration

- Jealousy

- Resentment

You may also find that you're beginning to reduce your efforts toward your commitment. You may be engaging in destructive behaviors and not following through on your commitment. These are all signs that your life may be out of balance.

Step back and take a deep breath if this happens. Assess your action plan. Is it too ambitious? Do you need to slow down a bit? Remember, we're not aiming for perfection but a consistent, persistent and positive path forward.

Ideally, your vision will include your ideas of a balanced life and you'll remember to leave time for those elements of your life that are important.

STOP!

Action Step #3

Spend some time evaluating what balance means to you. How much time do you spend on tasks that support you? How much time do you spend on tasks you dislike and/or that deplete you?

What changes can you make and how can your commitments support you to achieve a more balanced life?

There's something called the Law of Manifestation which states, "That which is like unto itself is drawn."

This simply means that we attract what we put out into the world. If you're positive, you'll attract positive people and experiences. If you are generous, you'll attract generosity.

You are responsible for what happens in your life. Whatever you focus on is what you invite in. That doesn't mean that bad things don't happen to good people. They do. However, the emotions that you focus on can and do invite more positive or negative emotions.

The Law of Manifestation can help you stay positive on the path toward honoring your commitment and taking consistent and positive action toward your purpose.

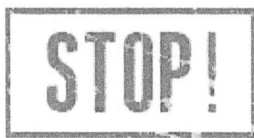

STOP!

Action Step #4

Assess how the Law of Manifestation has impacted your life. Take a look at successes that you've had. Did you have a positive outlook? Did you attract people to your cause or receive opportunities?

How were you able to create and/or take responsibility for opportunities and challenges that showed up in your life?

Spend some time exploring how to integrate the Law of Manifestation into your current commitments.

Full Speed Ahead

Jerry Rice is considered one of the greatest football players of all time and he was known to go the extra mile in everything he did. He'd come to practice an hour early every day and stay an extra hour afterwards to perfect his routes.

When Rice lined up it was as if he was playing in a real game. Jerry would take off at full speed and run his route to perfection. Once he caught the ball, even if it was a short route, he'd continue to run at full speed all the way to the end zone. Once he reached the end zone he'd turn around and run all the way back at full speed and hand the coach the ball. He ran every single route with precision, every time, every practice.

Jerry was once asked why he always ran at full speed to the end zone. He said, "When my hands touch the ball, I've trained my body to be in the end zone." Jerry always gave 100% and, no matter whether the 49ers were winning or losing, he would always perform at his highest level. That's why he's in the Pro Football Hall of Fame.

Like Jerry Rice, when you commit to anything, you must put in the extra effort and go the extra mile.

9

IT'S AS EASY AS A TWO-BY-FOUR

"Desire is the key to motivation, but it's determination and commitment to an unrelenting pursuit of your goal - a commitment to excellence - that will enable you to attain the success you seek."

— *Mario Andretti*

WALK THE PLANK

Most of us never really know the power of focus. There was an interesting motivational talk on this subject given by former Dallas Cowboys coach Jimmy Johnson:

"I told my players that if I laid a two-by four plank across the room, everybody there would walk across it and not fall, because our focus would be on walking that two-by-four. But if I put that same plank 10 stories high between two buildings, only a few would make it because the focus would be on falling. Focus is everything. The team that is more focused is the team that will win this game."

Johnson told them not to be distracted by the magnitude of the Super Bowl, but to focus on each play as if it were a good practice session. The Cowboys won 52-17.

You have established your commitment. You've created an action plan that incorporates your values, your concept of a balanced life and your resources. You may have even taken a step toward your end result.

How do you stay on track to achieve success? What tools do you have and what resources can you embrace to help you along the way? Let's look at some of the challenges you may come up against as well as some strategies you can utilize to help you succeed.

ACCOUNTABILITY PARTNER

An accountability partner is someone who supports you completely and can help you stay on track to achieve your goals and dreams. They may be someone whom you're close to, such as a spouse, friend or family member. It may also be someone who is going through a similar process, in which case you'd be their accountability partner as well.

An accountability partner can also be a coach. Coaches are wonderful resources because they're 100% dedicated to you. They can monitor you and your commitments without bias and they may have a broader view of what you're dealing with, unlike someone who is already close to you who may have some built-in biases and emotions.

Working with an accountability partner requires establishing some guidelines at the outset. How will you support one another? How will you connect and report your progress?

For example, will you meet once a month to discuss your progress and challenges and help motivate each other? Will you connect online on a weekly basis to share progress?

Working with an accountability partner can be quite effective. However, it has to be a supportive relationship and guidelines should be established to help create a mutually productive and positive experience.

STOP!

Action Step #1

Whom should you choose as an accountability partner and why? What type of system or structure might you set up? You could create a group of people, such as a Mastermind Group, to help one another stay accountable, motivated and on track.

Write the script that you'll use to ask someone to be your accountability partner. What would you

say? How would you ask them to support you and
what do you have to offer in return?

COMMITMENT BOOK

A commitment book is a success journal of sorts.
You can use an actual notebook and a pen to track your
daily progress. You might, for example, sit down after
dinner and record what you did today that pushed you
closer to your goal and helped you follow through on
your commitment.

SPREADSHEETS AND CHECKLISTS

You can also print out a series of checklists and check
off your daily activities. Or, if you prefer spreadsheets or
electronic documentation, you can create a document on
your computer that helps you track your daily progress.

VISUALIZATION BOARD

Some people prefer to represent their progress by
cutting items out of magazines and pasting them onto
a large poster board. Create a few boards to represent
the path or a single board to symbolize your ideal life.

Because most people are visual like i am, I use a tool, which I call my Daily Method of Operation (DMO). Without this, it's difficult to see my success or my failures. The DMO gives me a quick visual of whether I am moving towards success or I am moving towards failure. I have daily actions that need to be done each day in order to accomplish my commitment.

For each day that I have completed my tasks I color a corner of the diagram up and over to the right. If I did not do all or any one of the daily actions I color a box down and to the right.

MONTHLY COMMITMENT SUCCESS TRACKER

My Daily Method of Operations

For the month of _____

MONTHLY COMMITMENT SUCCESS TRACKER

My Daily Method of Operations

For the month of _____

You can download the DMO doc at www.ManagingYourCommitmentToSuccess.com/downloads

STOP!

Action Step #2

Identify a means to visualize and track your commitments. Use the method for a week or two and decide if it's the right system for you.

REVIEW YOUR COMMITMENTS DAILY

Whichever method you choose, make sure that you create some sort of system to review your commitments on a daily basis. Some people prefer to wake in the morning and review what's in store for them that day. They create morning rituals to embrace the day, remember their values, and to focus on their path.

Others prefer to conclude the day by taking a look at their progress, expressing gratitude for success and evaluating what they must do the next day. They're then able to go to bed with clarity.

NEVER STOP PLANNING

The daily review process is a means to evaluate how your plans are working out. It's quite likely that you'll need to adapt and change your plans as you go. For example, if you're going back to school and your financial aid falls through, you may need to modify your plans.

Continually assessing your commitments and your plans helps you adapt more quickly and stay on the path of success.

Finally, let's not forget that there's joy when you keep your commitment.

This magic isn't just experienced at the end when it's all said and done; it's experienced throughout the entire process. This is one of the reasons it's so important to make commitment-keeping part of your daily routine. When you can step back and assess your day and your progress, you realize just how wonderful and powerful commitment keeping really is.

Tracking your progress and making regular assessments of your success is just one of the ways to enjoy the journey. Another is to reward yourself along the way. Take time to celebrate your progress. Reward yourself for keeping your commitment and have fun.

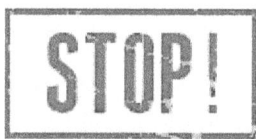

STOP!

Action Step #3

Decide how you're going to reward yourself along the way. Review your action plan and timeline and identify rewards for each milestone. Make it something simple like a dinner, a movie or a coffee shop treat.

Create a final "big bang" type of reward to celebrate achieving your long-term goal and commitment. When the days get rough and challenges feel insurmountable, the rewards waiting for you at the end of the road (even the intangible ones) will help you stay motivated to follow through and succeed.

CLEARING THE INTERNAL CLUTTER

Have you ever found yourself frozen in time, having spent hours in front of your computer, unable to account for anything that you did? If you've been spinning your wheels, it could be for a couple of reasons. Either you were trying to do too many things at once or you were concentrating on insignificant tasks and putting off the work you really need to do. Often we take on too many things and we don't finish any of them.

What's your routine? When you get to your computer, do you check your e-mail, Facebook, and Twitter or answer calls? Unless there's something urgent that you know is pending, this is a waste of your best time.

Your first responsibility is to get into the right mindset. In order to be successful, you must take action. Sounds simple, right? Then why is it so hard to do? Often it's because the tasks are boring or difficult. The problem is that denial won't cause the task to go away.

1. **Take a look at your thinking.** If your mind is full of negative thoughts, you will start to believe that the task is impossible and that it's OK to give up, put it off or leave it unfinished. Instead of thinking, "I can't do this," tell yourself, "I will get this done now."

2. **Get to know when your peak performance time is.** Choose that time to do your task if it's urgent or important.

3. **Make the main thing the main thing.** Decide what your most important tasks are and do them first. It isn't rude to ignore your email. Prioritize and take responsibility for what you need to do.

4. **Learn to say no.** Many times it's hard to say no, either because we don't want to let somebody down or because we're afraid to turn jobs away. But if we overextend ourselves, we might not have any jobs to finish. Most clients will respect an honest no and appreciate your time if you are too busy.

5. **Be careful about distractions.** People may come to you and say, "I just have a quick question," and that might be true. But if 20 people come to you with a quick question, your day is used up with other people's work.

6. **Learn to make decisions.** Some people train themselves to do this by setting a stopwatch. They give themselves one minute to make a decision and then move on.

7. **Don't forget to treat yourself.** No matter how hard we work on our mindset, there will always

be some tasks we just don't like. There's nothing wrong with a bribe for completing the things we don't like to do.

8. **Take a look at the time you waste when you're away from work.** What do you do when you're shopping, driving, or standing in lines? Do you fill that time with worrying or negative thoughts? Instead, train your mind to be thinking about new things you can do for your business.

9. **Don't overwhelm yourself.** Come to understand what you can reasonably accomplish in a certain period of time and make that your goal. Break it down into steps so that you won't be overwhelmed in the process.

10. **For tasks that you find especially daunting or unpleasant,** make use of a simple kitchen timer. Set it for 30 minutes and work as intensely as you can on the project. Then take a break and work on something else for a while.

DRIVERS THAT KEEP US STUCK

There are certain things called drivers that keep us stuck. Most of us have one or more of them, and they are the enemies of productivity. They can cause damage to our feelings, our relationships, our self-esteem and even our health. They can wreak havoc with our business. But when we know what they are, our self-talk can tame them and even banish them. See if any of these drivers apply to you.

THE BE PERFECT DRIVER

The idea that we should be perfect is pervasive in our society. We berate ourselves and expect 100% perfection, no matter what the task is. Often, if we don't think we can be perfect, we do nothing at all. Since most of us are generally less-than-perfect at most things, it becomes a lose-lose situation. It can be paralyzing and debilitating, and it can keep us from achieving the things we want most. Alcohol, drugs, or overeating are often side effects of someone suffering from the Be Perfect driver.

THE BE STRONG DRIVER

The Be Strong driver regards any need as a weakness to be overcome. The driver says that you must do it all yourself and you must not ask for help from anyone.

Feelings of sadness or hurt or loneliness, or "weak" feelings, are unacceptable. They are humiliating feelings which we must hide.

THE HURRY UP DRIVER

The Hurry Up driver pushes us to do more and more, faster and faster. This trap makes us impatient with ourselves and others. It can impede our productivity with us either not being able to meet tight deadlines or meeting them at the risk of our health and our relationships. We can all agree that the Hurry Up driver is becoming more prevalent in our society.

THE PLEASE OTHERS DRIVER

The Please Others driver demands that we are approved of above all else. People driven by this can feel anxiety and depression and intense fear of rejection even from people who are not important to them. These people have difficulty asserting their own needs. This can create problems such as over-promising and under-delivering.

THE TRY HARD DRIVER

At first, the Try Hard driver seems like a good thing. The problem is that it doesn't allow you to set limits on your trying. If there are no boundaries about how much you can help, how many things you can do, or how soon you can do them, the important things become obscured by all the things you've committed yourself to. There's simply not enough time for everything.

Drivers are a paradox. We think they're helping us and we think we're behaving correctly. In actuality, they cause us to accomplish little or nothing, much less than if we took a step back, saw them for the negative forces they are, applied some self-talk and took control of the situation.

LEARNING TO FOCUS

In *The Four Hour Work Week*, Timothy Ferriss wrote a chapter on time management in which he tells us to forget all about it. He asks us five questions:

1. If you had a heart attack and could only work two hours per day, what would you do?

2. If you have a second heart attack and could only work two hours per week, what would you do?

3. If you had a gun to your head and had to stop doing 4/5ths of your different time-consuming activities, which would you remove?

4. What are the top three activities that you use to fill time to feel as though you've been productive?

5. Learn to ask, "If this is the only thing I accomplished today, will you be satisfied with my day?"

While Ferriss may not have a lot of respect for time management, he has a great deal of respect for focus. All five of his questions are attempting to get his readers to focus on the important things and minimize or completely eliminate the unimportant things.

The point he's making is about focus. We need to take a fresh honest look at our commitments and make the main thing the main thing.

DEVELOPING THE 5 POWERS

The most successful people share certain secrets or traits. People with power, success or money seem to have these things in common:

1. The power of persistence

2. The power of passion

3. The power of self-control

4. The power of decision and action

5. The power of creativity

THE POWER OF PERSISTENCE

We all know and admire people who have failed but still gone on to great success. Before he invented the electric light bulb, Thomas Edison failed more than 10,000 times. He never saw it as a failure; he saw it as one more step towards succeeding. Henry Ford came from a poor background with no education, but he looked at the horse and buggy and imagined the amazing cars we drive today. Abraham Lincoln failed several times, but we all know how he ended up. Persistence will carry you when intelligence and luck do not.

THE POWER OF PASSION

You've probably heard the expression, "If you can believe it, you can achieve it." A good idea alone is not enough. You have to believe in it. I'll bet you know people who are very intelligent but have never risen very high in life. I'll also bet you know other people who haven't had much going for them but have succeeded in spite of obstacles. It's very likely due to their determination to achieve their goals in spite of anything that comes against them. To the extent that you can acquire this attitude, you will succeed.

THE POWER OF SELF-CONTROL

The power of self-control in business is really about the way you handle your thoughts and your emotions. As you take action instead of procrastinate, manage drivers that keep you stuck, and learn to focus, you will enjoy success.

THE POWER OF DECISION AND ACTION

One of the greatest causes of failure is lack of decisiveness. Procrastination holds people back from achieving their full potential. Millionaires make decisions promptly, changing them only when necessary.

THE POWER OF CREATIVITY

So much of your success will depend on how creative your solutions are. If you can't think for yourself and imagine possibilities, you must depend only on what others before you have done. That might not be your best.

At its best, your plan of action will combine all these "success" qualities or traits to create a completely rewarding plan for yourself.

Now that we've cleared out the mental clutter and set up a positive mindset, we'll begin to clear out the clutter from your business with some practical steps and specific checklists.

1. Prioritize your tasks

Some people say that it's best to get your hardest task out of the way at the beginning of the day when you have the most energy. If you feel like you've accomplished something big, you'll be less stressed as the day goes on. Others like to finish a list of small jobs first and build momentum as the day goes on. The more they cross off their to-do list, the more productive and confident they feel. Try both ways to see which one motivates you.

2. Use calendars or daily planners

Decide what type of system you're going to use and then find a calendar or planner that matches that system. You can use traditional paper and pen, or you could use a phone or web-based app. Remember, though, calendars and planners only work if you use them. When used correctly, it won't take long before using a planner, or in our case, a Daily Method of Operation (DMO), becomes second nature.

3. Limit your distractions

You are probably painfully aware of all the distractions we are constantly tempted by, including Facebook, Twitter, instant messaging, email and computer games. You have to rely on your own self-discipline to limit those things so that you can get your important tasks completed. This is where your Daily Commitment Productivity Planner comes in handy.

4. Set a specific time when you can work on less important tasks

Less important tasks can be distractions, but it doesn't mean they don't need to be taken care of. If you have lots of discipline, you can intersperse things like e-mail or phone calls throughout your day. But if you tend to talk for long periods of time, you may need to save phone calls until after important jobs are finished.

If you find it almost impossible to hit the delete key when you're going through your email, you probably don't want to start your day with that. Email can act like a bright shiny object and make you fear that you're missing something if you don't open every one. If that's a weak area for you, allow yourself to take care of it only for a short amount of time.

5. Automate your tasks

Your time is valuable, and one of the easiest ways to gain more time is to automate routine tasks. If you're a writer, you might really like dictating your articles into voice recognition software. Think about tasks that you do frequently and investigate the technology that might help you with them.

6. Organize your desk and computer files

These tasks might seem daunting depending on the condition of your files, but they are well worth the time investment. You will save countless frustrating hours once your files are properly labeled. This is probably even more true for the files in your computer than it is for the files on your desk. If it seems like a huge task to tackle, work on one part at a time or work for 15 minutes each day until all your files are in order.

7. Use headphones to block out noise

This might seem trivial, but if you're working around a lot of noise your concentration can suffer. Noise canceling headphones or even earplugs can make a big difference.

8. Get a comfortable chair and good lighting

Are you really comfortable with your office chair and your lighting? Something that might seem trivial can have a huge impact on your productivity. It makes a difference in how you think, feel and perform. You might have been uncomfortable for so long that you don't even realize it. You owe it to yourself to be as comfortable as possible.

9. Clean up your workspace

Again, we're talking about the obvious. But the truth is it's much easier to stay focused when your workspace is clean and organized. Just looking at piles of junk can make you tense and wading through stacks of paper to find what you need is frustrating. Set up a method to store similar things together and put things in their proper places each time you use them.

10. Throw things out!

For some of us, throwing things out is almost impossible, but look at how much it costs you to hang on to those outdated, worn-out useless things. If you see them getting in the way of your productivity, it should be easier to let them go. If they have any usefulness left, sell them online or donate them.

WHY TIME MANAGEMENT?

Goal setting, to-do lists, limiting activities, prioritizing and outsourcing—it all seems like a lot MORE to do, not a time management plan. So let's review why you should practice time management anyway.

1. **It's Easy To Do** — Once your system is in place, it frees up much of your time. The techniques are easy to learn and inexpensive. In fact, lots of them are free.

2. **Your Personal Life Will Benefit** — One of the casualties of poor time management is personal or family time. Getting more done in less time gives you more time and money for the family.

3. **More Productivity** — Properly managed time means less time wasted. More time spent on important items means more productivity and success.

4. **Better Self-Esteem** — Remember the old joke, "Why are you beating your head against that wall?" Answer: "Because it feels so good when I stop." Enough said.

5. **More Options, A Better Life** — The better you manage your work life, the closer you get to the life you dream of.

"The only limit to your impact is your imagination and commitment."
- Anthony Robbins

MIKE DRIGGERS

10

HONOR YOUR COMMITMENT

"Success is not final, failure is not fatal: it is the
courage to continue that counts."
— *Winston Churchill*

GET OFF THE BRANCH!

There once was a king who was presented a gift
of two magnificent falcons. He gave them to a
falconer to be trained. Months passed before the
falconer informed the king that one of the falcons was
flying majestically and soaring high in the sky but the
other bird hadn't moved from its branch since the day
it had arrived.

The king summoned healers and sorcerers from all
over the land to tend to the falcon but no one could make
it fly. After trying everything he could, the king thought
to himself, "Maybe I need someone more familiar with

the countryside to understand the nature of this problem." So the king told his servants, "Go and get a farmer."

The next day the second falcon was soaring high above the palace gardens. The king told his court, "Bring me the man behind this miracle." The farmer was brought to the king and was asked, "How did you make the falcon fly?" With his head bowed, the farmer said to the king, "It was very easy, your highness. I simply cut the branch where the bird was sitting."

The moral of this story? We are all made to fly. But to realize YOUR incredible potential, the branch needs to be cut.

Every single day I see smart and capable people sitting on their branches, clinging to the things that are familiar to them. They never take that leap of faith to soar high in business and in life.

The possibilities are endless, but for most people they remain undiscovered. We conform to the familiar, the comfortable and the mundane. Don't live MEDIOCRE lives! Make them exciting, thrilling and fulfilling.

You've come a long way just by finishing this book but you don't have to stop here. You'll continue to face hurdles and possibly even some resistance from those who can't handle your new success, but persistence will pay off handsomely.

Start small, one commitment at a time. Create a pattern of success and learn what trips you up and how you overcome challenges. The success you achieve will snowball into more success. Who you become and the things you will accomplish will allow you to live the life you desire - the life you truly deserve when you learn the secret of Managing Your Commitment to Success.

SEE WHERE YOU'RE GOING

On July 4, 1952, a young woman named Florence Chadwick waded into the water off Catalina Island. On that fog covered morning, she intended to swim the channel from the island to the California coast.

Florence wasn't a rookie; she was the first woman to swim the English Channel in both directions. But the water was numbing cold that morning and the fog was so thick she could hardly see two feet in front of her. Several times, sharks had to be driven away with rifle fire from the boats in her party.

She swam for more than fifteen hours before she asked to be taken out of the water. Her trainer coaxed her to swim on since they were so close to land, but all Florence saw ahead was the thick fog. She quit only half a mile from her goal.

Later she said, "I'm not excusing myself, but if I could have seen the land, I might have made it."

Florence didn't fail because of fear, exhaustion or the cold water. It was the fog.

Two months after her failed attempt at swimming the length of the channel, Florence waded into the water off the same beach on Catalina Island, swam the full distance and set a new speed record — all because she could clearly see her goal.

CONCLUSION

*"We are what we repeatedly do. Excellence,
therefore, is not an act but a habit."*
— *Aristotle*

If we're honest with ourselves, this quote will resonate within. We are most known by what we do, not what we say. If we are consistent in our actions and our work ethic, people take notice. Success is a measure of doing the common things uncommonly well. Don't do a good job, do a great job! Consistently successful behavior translates to excellence.

Truly successful people have integrity, a strong work ethic, a desire to succeed and the tenacity to keep working even when things aren't going well. They don't give up easily; they keep moving forward, regardless of how many times they're knocked back.

I have been through some incredible life events. I have had great success and more than a few failures with my dreams and projects. The principles in this book are the lessons that I have learned and adapted to my life to help me succeed. Two things I agree on, you miss all the shots you don't take and there is no traffic on the freeway of greatness.

Make sure to always be honest with yourself. Work hard. Don't give up. Be consistent and persistent. Do a great job with everything you commit to and enter every commitment with success on your mind.

Don't wait for success to come to you. Be proactive to ensure that you attain the success you desire. Take the initiative to do more than is expected of you each day. Be excellent in your work. Then, when the opportunity presents itself, make the most of it. Ask yourself everyday, "Am I consistent in my actions? Do I do my best work each and every day? Am I providing my commitment to excellence rather than mediocrity? Am I doing more than is expected?"

If you can answer yes to all those questions, you are truly Managing Your Commitment.

ABOUT THE AUTHOR

Mike Driggers Is a Top selling author, International in demand celebrity speaker, the world's leading Authority Marketing Agent^{tm}, consultant, business owner and master strategist who inspires, motivates, and empowers people worldwide. Mike has been featured on ABC, NBC, FOX, CBS, PBS, USA Today, Business Journal, Wall Street Journal and the Brian Tracy Show. Mike is recognized as one of the world's most requested business, sales & marketing consultant. He is an in-demand international celebrity business and motivational keynote speaker who has delivered over 2500 presentations worldwide. Mike consistently wows audiences with his entertaining and interactive keynotes, seminars, workshops, coaching, and training programs.

Mike is the author of several books titled "Mastering of The Mind Set", "Unleash The Intrapreneurship Within", "Nothing in LIFE Starts Until YOU Start", "Nothing in SALES Starts Until YOU Start" and "Nothing in LEADER-SHIP Starts Until YOU Start" "Managing Your Commitment". Mike has also co-authored several books titled "Entrepreneurs On Fire" with Barbara Corcoran from the hit TV series, The Shark Tank, "Reach Your Greatness" with James Malinchak from the featured hit ABC TV Show Secret Millionaire", "On Target Marketing" with Vince Baker co-owner of On Target Marketing Group.

Mike has shared the stage with many great thought leaders like James Malinchak, Brain Tracy, Jon Assaraf, Jack Canfield, Zig Ziglar, Jim Rohn, Les Brown, Loral Langemeier, Rudy Ruettiger, Eric Worre, Jeff Olson, Kevin Harrington, Forbes Riley, Glenn Morshower, Seth Godin, Jill Lublin, Kevin Clayson, Richard Kaye, Joel Comm, Darin Adams, Craig Duswalt, Trish Carr, Berny Dohrmann, Shane Gibson, Seth Greene, David Hancock, Sharon Lechter, Nancy Matthews, Ken McArthur, Nick Nanton, Greg S. Reid, E. Brian Rose, and much more.

Mike has been in the top 10% of producers for the direct sales industry for more than 30 years. Mike has owned and operated several successful businesses, including a Bay Area marketing and advertising agency called Unleashed Media where In 2004, he was voted entrepreneur of the year in his local area by President Bush.

Mike uses a no-nonsense, highly focused and disciplined

approach to creating real results quickly. He covers subjects including entrepreneurship, mindset, leadership, sales, marketing, high performance, and motivation. Mike's passion, desire, and willingness to be a servant leader has inspired and helped thousands of people achieve greatness within their personal and business lives. As a consultant, Mike's is a behind-the-scenes, go-to sales, marketing and leadership advisor for many businesses. His clientele is a Who's Who in the fields of sports, business, entertainment, and politics. He has helped people from all walks of life create amazing results quickly and hit top ranks within their business and careers. Vist www.BookMikeToday.com

NOTES:

NOTES:

PROCRASTINATION KILLER
Special **FREE** Bonus Gift For **YOU!**

To help you stand out from the crowd
FREE BONUS RESOURCE for you at;
www.theprocrastinationkiller.com/procrastinationgift

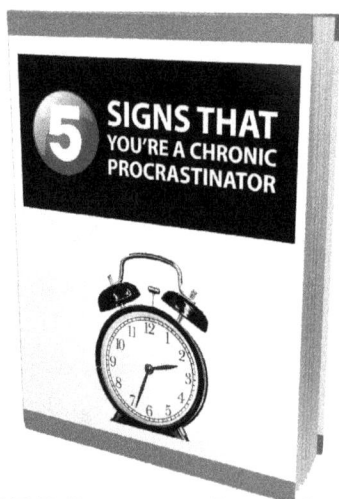

5 SIGNS THAT YOU'RE A CHRONIC PROCRASTINATOR

Get your FREE Report And You'll Discover...

1. The Top 5 most common signs of chronic procrastinators (It could be YOU!)

2. The reasons why you're terribly UNPRODUCTIVE!

3. Your inner power to push through any procrastination pitfall

**www.theprocrastinationkiller.com/
procrastinationgift**

THE IDEAL PROFESSIONAL SPEAKER FOR Your NEXT EVENT!

Any organization that wants to develop and grow their business to become "extraordinary" needs to hire Mike for a keynote and /or workshop training!

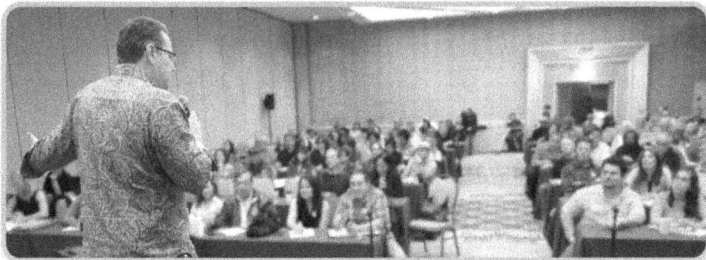

TO CONTACT OR BOOK MIKE TO SPEAK:

IME Publishing Group

(866) 7BOOKME

(866) 726-6563

www.BookMikeToday.com

Info@BookMikeToday.com

www.ingramcontent.com/pod-product-compliance
Lightning Source LLC
Chambersburg PA
CBHW050020100426
42739CB00011B/2719